MAKING THE CONNECTION

Language and Academic Achievement Among African American Students

Carolyn Temple Adger
Donna Christian
Orlando Taylor
Editors

Proceedings of a conference of the
Coalition on Language Diversity in Education

A publication of the
Center for Applied Linguistics and

Prepared by the
inghouse on Languages

, Inc

CΛL   ERIC®

Printed in the United States of America
10 9 8 7 6 5 4 3 2 1

Language in Education 92

Editorial/production supervision: Jeanne Rennie
Copyediting: Jeanne Rennie
Editorial assistance: Sonia Kundert, Amy Fitch, and Richard A. Bryant
Design and production: Sonia Kundert
Cover: SAGARTdesign

ISBN 1-887744-42-8

Library of Congress Cataloging-in-Publication Data
Making the connection : language and academic achievement among African
    American students : proceedings of a conference of the Coalition on Language
    Diversity in Education / Carolyn Temple Adger, Donna Christian, Orlando L.
    Taylor, editors.
        p.   cm. -- (Language in education ; 92)
    Includes bibliographical references (p.   ) and index.
    ISBN 1-887744-42-8 (pbk.)
    1. Afro-American students--Education--Congresses.   2. Language arts--
United States--Congresses.   3. Academic achievement--United States--
Congresses.   4. Black English--United States--Congresses.   5. Afro-Americans--
Languages.   6. Language and education--United States.   I. Adger, Carolyn
Temple.   II. Christian, Donna.   III. Taylor, Orlando L.   IV. Coalition on
Language Diversity in Education.   V. Center for Applied Linguistics.   VI.
ERIC Clearinghouse on Languages and Linguistics.   VII. Series.
LC2778.L34M35   1999
427'.973'08996073--dc21   98-52017
                                                                                CIP

Contents

Preface   v

Chapter 1
**Language Diversity and Academic Achievement in the Education
of African American Students—An Overview of the Issues**   1
  John R. Rickford

Chapter 2
**The Language of African American Students
in Classroom Discourse**   31
  Courtney B. Cazden

Chapter 3
Enhancing Bidialectalism in Urban African American Students   53
  Kelli Harris-Wright

Chapter 4
**Repercussions From the Oakland Ebonics Controversy—
The Critical Role of Dialect Awareness Programs**   61
  Walt Wolfram

Chapter 5
Considerations in Preparing Teachers for Linguistic Diversity   81
  John Baugh

Chapter 6
The Case for Ebonics As Part of Exemplary Teacher Preparation   97
  Terry Meier

Chapter 7
Language Policy and Classroom Practices   115
  Geneva Smitherman

Chapter 8
**Language, Diversity, and Assessment—
Ideology, Professional Practice, and the Achievement Gap**   125
  Asa G. Hilliard, III

Chapter 9
**Lessons Learned From the Ebonics Controversy—
Implications for Language Assessment**   137
  Anna F. Vaughn-Cooke

Appendix
Testimony of Orlando L. Taylor on the Subject of "Ebonics"   169

About the Authors   177
About the Editors   179

Preface

Variation in the English language at any level—pronunciation, grammar, vocabulary, discourse style—often provokes comment. People may be curious, pleased, or disapproving of others' ways of speaking, depending on which variety of English is being used and in what setting. But the pervasiveness and intensity of public discussion about the Oakland, CA, School Board's December 1996 policy concerning language variation was unprecedented. Suddenly, intrinsic beliefs about language in schools were being expressed and broadcast widely, exposing fundamental misunderstandings about language variation in the United States. Unwarranted claims regarding the nature of variation and appropriate educational responses proliferated without adequate critique in public and private conversation. In response, leaders of national organizations concerned with issues of language diversity in education determined to address this situation together. They formed a coalition committed to leading a coherent, informed response to the Ebonics controversy that would support excellence and equity in the education of Ebonics speakers and other African American students. The Coalition on Language Diversity in Education has 13 members:

- American Association for Applied Linguistics
- American Dialect Society
- American Speech-Language-Hearing Association
- Center for Applied Linguistics
- Council of the Great City Schools
- Howard University's Graduate School of Arts and Sciences
- Linguistic Society of America
- National Alliance of Black School Educators
- National Black Association for Speech-Language and Hearing
- National Communication Association
- National Council of Teachers of English
- Office of Educational Research and Improvement, U.S. Department of Education
- Teachers of English to Speakers of Other Languages

In January 1998, the Coalition sponsored a national invitational conference, *Language Diversity and Academic Achievement in the Education of African American Students*, that brought together some 50 national leaders in language, education, and public policy. In presentations and group discussions, conference participants articulated their views of what the United States must do to meet the academic needs of African American students, as well as those of other students with respect to language variation. They outlined essential dimensions of programs and policies and cited research that provides a solid basis for continuing investigation.

This volume presents the proceedings of that conference. In chapter 1, John Rickford's overview suggests what we need to do to address language issues in the education of African American students: recognize the scope and nature of the problem, including its non-linguistic components; improve teachers' and students' attitudes toward and knowledge about African American Vernacular English (AAVE), or Ebonics; improve the teaching of Standard English; and improve the teaching of speaking, reading, and writing. The chapters that follow his overview address five domains in which various dimensions of language use, including the differences between standard dialects and vernacular dialects, affect the education of Ebonics speakers: classroom discourse (chapter 2), the school curriculum (chapters 3 and 4), teacher education (chapters 5 and 6), language policy (chapter 7), and testing (chapters 8 and 9).

Language Variation and Education—What Do We Know and What Do We Need to Know?

A substantial body of sociolinguistic research describes the features of African American Vernacular English (AAVE) that differentiate it from other dialects of English. The regular, predictable occurrence of these features defines AAVE (also known as Ebonics) as one of many varieties of the English language, not a faulty version of an idealized English, as some see it. Other research in sociolinguistics, as well as in education, anthropological linguistics, sociology, social psychology, and speech/language pathology, sheds light on discourse dimensions of speaking and writing by Ebonics speakers. The contributors to this volume remind us of the potential of this research to explain the linguistic performance of African American students and to support their educational achievement. But, as many of them argue, this potential has barely been acknowledged, let alone mined, because of unwarranted beliefs about language and because of disciplinary traditions, indifference, and racism.

Classroom discourse

Reviewing research on variation in language structure and style in classroom discourse (chapter 2), Courtney Cazden points out that classroom talk assumes greater importance in the current understanding of how cognitive development occurs and in some of the high stakes testing associated with school reform. Educators' attitudes toward language differences thus have an increased potential to influence educational outcomes: Positive attitudes reinforce opportunities for students to build on the language skills they bring to school; negative attitudes increase the risks often associated with language differences.

Conference participants agreed with Cazden that we need to know more about language use in classrooms and about students' opportunities to participate academically. In particular, we need to know more about the ways in which teachers' behavior influences students' talk. We need research on how teachers gain expertise in language variation and language use, how their own language backgrounds and ethnicity affect that, and how expanded teacher expertise supports student achievement.

Curriculum and instruction

Issues in Ebonics and the educational achievement of African American students cut across the school curriculum, as Cazden's and Rickford's chapters emphasize, because oral language and literacy are intrinsic to learning mathematics, science, social studies, literature, and the rest. Yet the Ebonics debate has correctly highlighted a particular curricular area that demands development—the teaching of Standard English. Oakland's intention to do just that touched off the national firestorm suggesting public demand for this curricular focus if not agreement on goals and methods. Schools have been teaching standard English but using traditional methods that ignore or trivialize research on language variation. Resources are limited, and teachers are not sufficiently knowledgeable about crucial details. There is little research on pedagogical methods. But the new Standard

English curricula that are being developed, tried out, and evaluated use contrastive analysis approaches that make dialect contrasts clear, as Rickford suggests they should (chapter 1). The DeKalb County (GA) school system's bidialectal curriculum, which Kelli Harris-Wright describes in chapter 3, is one of these. Conference participants agreed that we need much more research and development to support programs like this one. We need to learn how teachers understand the process of developing proficiency in a standard dialect and how they promote it. We need to know more about how language diversity pertains to learning in the content areas and how it can be accommodated.

Teachers' obligations to Ebonics speakers are not exhausted by supporting their development of Standard English, even when that is done in ways that respect and make use of the students' Ebonics proficiency, as does the program Harris-Wright describes. Walt Wolfram (chapter 4) urges expansion of the typically vestigial approach to dialect knowledge in the school curriculum by introducing students to the facts of language variation through scientific methods: examining language data, forming hypotheses about patterns, and testing them against more data. The program he outlines, which is appropriate for language arts, social studies, and cross-disciplinary study, would not only update the curriculum but also combat the dialect stereotypes so shockingly evident in most discussions about Ebonics.

Teacher education

At present, however, it appears that few teachers are prepared to teach students about language variation or even to respond to evidence of it in ways that support students' language development and academic achievement. Among conference participants, there was consensus that education for teachers about language and language variation is simply inadequate. As John Baugh points out (chapter 5), institutions that prepare teachers often fail to provide courses that give detailed information about language variation and about students' dialects. There are few materials about the effects of language and dialect diversity in education for teacher educators to use themselves and as texts for teachers. There are even fewer for classroom teachers to use with their students. Promising approaches, such as those discussed by Terry Meier in chapter 6, are not yet widely used. But both

Baugh and Meier point out that as important as linguistic education is for teachers, information alone will not solve all the problems of linguistic bias in education. Attitudes must be examined. Baugh points also to universities' failure to support teacher education as fully as they do other professions.

Echoing Cazden (chapter 2), Meier provides examples of what can happen in schools when teachers dismiss their students' cultural backgrounds, interpreting differences as deficits. They are likely to overlook or discount children's language strengths and to create instructional settings that do not engage students linguistically or cognitively. Meier argues that teachers need to learn about African American literary traditions in order to help their students build literacy from oracy.

To build teachers' and teacher interns' capacity to support language and literacy development in vernacular speakers, we need detailed descriptions of approaches that work and answers to related questions. Can these approaches be supported through collaboration across university departments and between schools and universities? What is the ultimate effect on student achievement when teachers appreciate a wider range of language skills than those used in their own communities? We need long-term applied research that documents the process of developing and institutionalizing more effective programs on language in education and their ultimate effects on teaching and learning in the schools.

Language policy

The weaknesses in educational practice concerning dialects of English continue to exist because they are tolerated, not because of an impoverished research base on which solutions can be built, nor because policy is lacking. Geneva Smitherman profiles U.S. language policy regarding language variation (chapter 7), presenting in full the National Language Policy developed by the Conference on College Composition and Communication (CCCC), an affiliate of the National Council of Teachers of English (NCTE). Some of the other, outdated language policies that she mentions saw new life in Ebonics diatribes—evidence that a research-based, practice-informed language policy such as that of the CCCC is needed at every level of education to undergird a more linguistically realistic, practical language education for U.S. citizens.

Tests and measurement

The last two chapters confront the persistence of linguistically naive testing that discounts the abilities of vernacular dialect speakers. In chapter 8, Asa Hilliard recounts his experiences seeking fairness in assessment and mental measurement by challenging the assumptions of universality on which testing and measurement rest. He points to linguistic differences, such as syntactic contrasts among varieties of English; to psychometric constructs, such as basic word lists that are incorrectly assumed to be invariant across social groups; and to testing conditions that may have different meanings for different groups. In chapter 9, Fay Vaughn-Cooke points out that testing and placement in speech/language pathology services is conducted by professionals whose views of language are influenced by the same language attitudes that revealed themselves in the Ebonics debate. She asserts that linguists' attempts to present facts to a poorly informed public are largely futile, because myths about language variation, and about Ebonics speakers in particular, may be impervious to science. She concurs with Smitherman (chapter 7) and Baugh (chapter 5) that science must partner with policy.

Congressional testimony

The volume closes with Orlando Taylor's testimony to the United States Senate Committee on Appropriations, Subcommittee on Labor, Health and Human Services and Education, delivered within the first month of the Ebonics debate. It captures the essence of language scholars' reactions, formulated for policy makers but suitable for the public.

Partners in the Walk to Equity

The chapters in this volume explicate important language issues in the educational achievement of African American students. They also point out dimensions of a necessary program of research and development to solve problems of educational inequity due to language prejudice. The Coalition on Language Diversity in Education, the authors of these chapters, and other conference participants are engaged in a walk to the linguistic freedom that Smitherman (chapter 5) mentions—a state in which everyone's language is honored in fact and every student's academic achievement is supported. This volume advances us a step in our walk. It is offered as a resource for others in the partnership—schools, school districts, boards of education, schools of education, state and federal departments of education, parents, students, and others who share the vision of educational excellence for linguistically diverse African American children and for all children in our schools today.

Carolyn Temple Adger
Donna Christian
Orlando Taylor
Washington, DC
July 1, 1998

Language Diversity and Academic Achievement in the Education of African American Students— An Overview of the Issues[1]

John R. Rickford

Why consider this issue now? Why consider it at all? Despite the commendable generality and neutrality of its title, the driving force behind the conference whose proceedings are included in this volume is the furor that erupted in December 1996 when the Oakland (CA) School Board resolved to recognize Ebonics as the "primary language of African American students" and to take it into account in facilitating "their acquisition and mastery of English language skills."

The first question one might ask is why hold a conference on this issue one year after the furor erupted, and why publish a book on it two years afterward, when the issue has long since lost the attention of the media and the public? The reason for this is simply that the crisis that led Oakland to its radical resolution in 1996—the fact that (primarily working-class) African American students were performing more poorly in school than students from virtually every other ethnicity, particularly in the central areas of reading and writing—remains unchanged (see section 2 below). Moreover, the crisis is not confined to Oakland or California; it is evident in school districts across the United States. The teachers and parents of these students cannot give up on the issue simply because the television crews and reporters have packed up and gone away. They must continue to search for deeper understandings and solutions. There is evidence that the vernacular of African American students (called Ebonics or African American Vernacular English [AAVE]) can be used to help them improve their skills in reading and the language arts and do better in school more generally. Ebonics is by no means a panacea for *all* the problems that beset African American students in schools, but it is potentially part of the solution and from that perspective alone deserves consideration.

The second question some might ask is why hold a conference with this focus at all? At a point in history when so many people have struggled to overcome differential opportunity and treatment by race (i.e., discrimination) in education, employment, housing, and other areas, do we really need to zero in on the problems facing African American students, as if they were somehow different from other students and as if the principles of good teaching somehow did not apply to them? This sentiment was widely echoed when the Ebonics firestorm erupted. For instance, the poet Maya Angelou, despite her own use of Ebonics in such poems as "The Thirteens" and "The Pusher,"[2] was quoted in *USA Today* (December 23, 1996) as saying that she was "incensed" by Oakland's Ebonics resolution and found it "very threatening, because it can encourage young men and women not to learn standard English." Similarly, Jim Boulet, executive director of the national organization English First, felt that the Oakland resolution was "saying in the most racist way that Black kids are stupid and they can't learn English, so let's not bother with that" (Diringer & Olszewski, 1996, p. A17).

The impression that Oakland was not interested in teaching Standard English (SE) was of course the most widespread misunderstanding throughout the Ebonics firestorm, the one that sent newspaper editorial and letter writers, TV commentators, radio callers, and talk show hosts into paroxysms of pontification about the importance of learning "proper" English. However, even those who recognized that Oakland was committed to teaching SE[3] objected to the suggestion that students' vernacular (Ebonics) had to be taken into account to help them learn SE. As an (African American) editor of a major U.S. trade book publisher wrote more recently:

> I find the whole notion of Ebonics counterproductive, condescending, and offensive. . . . The notion of using Ebonics to teach standard English implies that Black children aren't capable of learning standard English the way other children do. My parents were raised in the Jim Crow south by parents without high school degrees, and they managed to learn standard English without Ebonics even under those difficult conditions. (personal communication, December 5, 1997)[4]

In response to this, I would say that while I commend the successes of every individual African American (or other) student who masters Standard English and does well in school without special intervention,[5] and while I agree that the very best principles of teaching and learning should be followed in the education of *all* students, the evidence that schools are failing massive numbers of African American students with existing methods is so overwhelming that it would be counterproductive and offensive to continue using them uncritically. To turn the powerful words of the Reverend Jesse Jackson on their head, to accept existing methods represents "an unconditional surrender, borderlining on disgrace"[6] (Lewis, 1996). Methods of teaching reading and writing that take the language diversity of African American students into account have shown greater promise than those that do not. Hence their relevance, and hence this conference and these proceedings.

In this overview, I address the following aspects of what I think we need to do in response to the crisis affecting African American students:

1. Recognize the scope of the problem.
2. Recognize the nature of the problem, including its several nonlinguistic components.
3. Improve teachers', students', and parents' attitudes and knowledge regarding Ebonics or AAVE.
4. Improve the teaching of Standard English.
5. Improve the teaching of writing and speaking more generally.
6. Improve the teaching of reading.

1. Recognize the scope of the problem—The devastating rate at which schools fail African American students.

Hutchison (1997), in a critique of the Oakland School Board and all "Ebonics advocates," points to statistics indicating that African Americans are not doing as badly in schools as some suggest:

> According to the National Urban League's State of Black America, 1995 report, nearly eighty percent of Blacks graduated from high school and nearly thirty-five percent were enrolled in college. (p. 37)

While it is important to recognize and applaud every achievement of this type, it is delusionary to pretend that a larger problem does not exist.

It was massive evidence of the problems facing African American students—the largest ethnic group in their school population—that led the Oakland School Board to create the Task Force on the Education of African American Students in 1996, and it was one of the recommendations of this task force that led the school board to its Ebonics resolution. The school board itself provided the relevant statistics as a supplement to the resolution, noting that although 53% of the 51,706 students in its school district were African American, only 35% of the students in Gifted and Talented Education were African American. By contrast, 71% of all students enrolled in special education were African American; 80% of all suspended students were African American; African American students had the lowest grade point average (1.80 or a C-) of all students in the district; and 19% of African American students who made it to the 12th grade did not graduate. The converse of this last statistic, incidentally, is what Hutchison cites with pride ("nearly eighty percent . . . graduated from high school"). But the non-graduation of one out of every five students is surely no cause for elation.

In the comparison of Black rates of school success with White rates, particularly on standardized measures of reading and writing, the full scope of the problem becomes clear. Consider, for instance, the 1989-90 test performances of third and sixth graders in the Palo Alto, California, School District (predominantly White, middle and upper-middle class) and in the adjacent Ravenswood School District (predominantly Black, working and under class), both about one hour's drive south of Oakland. The Palo Alto kids scored high on both reading and writing in third grade (96th and 94th percentiles respectively) and improved to the very top of the scale (the 99th percentile) by sixth grade, showing that the schools are able to build on whatever abilities children bring to school and add value to them before they leave. By contrast, the Ravenswood kids scored low on tests of reading and writing in third grade—in the 16th and 21st percentiles respectively—and declined even further, to the 3rd percentile (meaning only 2% of sixth graders statewide did worse), by sixth grade. This coincides with the very general finding reported by Steele (1992) that the longer African American students remain in school, the worse they do relative to mainstream (and particularly White) norms.

Pointing in the same direction is Michael Casserly's testimony before the U.S. Senate Appropriations Subcommittee on Labor, Health and Human Services, and Education on January 23, 1997, on the subject of Ebonics (*Ebonics*, 1997). Casserly, Executive Director of the Council of the Great City Schools (which includes 50 of the nation's largest urban public school districts), reported that in 1994, nine-year-old African American students were, on average, 29 points behind their White counterparts in reading proficiency (as measured on a 0 to 500-point scale). By the age of 13, the gap had increased to 31 points. By the age of 17, the gap was greater still, with African American students a full 37 points behind their White counterparts.[7] Casserly also reported that the 1992-93 scores of reading achievement by the 6 million inner-city children in Great City Schools indicate that while the percentage of White students scoring above the norm increased from 60.7% at the elementary level to 65.4% at the senior high level, the percentage of African American students scoring above the norm declined from 31.3% at the elementary level to 26.6% at the senior high level.[8]

2. Recognize the nature of the problem, including its several nonlinguistic components.

Linguists naturally concentrate on the linguistic aspects of such dramatic failure rates, including the differences between African American Vernacular English and the mainstream or Standard English that is expected and required in the schools. In this we are perfectly justified, but lest we forget the larger context of the problem and leave ourselves open to accusations of irrelevance or naïveté (Cose, 1997), we must recognize some of the other factors associated with the success or failure of schools in teaching and reaching African American students. Some of these factors may be more obvious than others, but all require increased study and understanding, as well as translation into teacher training, school funding, and policy making by school boards, counties, and state and federal legislative bodies. Some of these factors are described below.

School resources and facilities

The Reverend Jesse Jackson, discussing the Ebonics controversy on a visit to California at the end of December 1997, made the telling point that the average prison that houses primarily African Americans is better equipped than the average school that houses primarily African Americans. Freccia and Lau (1996) documented the disparity even more bleakly, noting, among other things, that

> in 1995, for the first time ever, California spent as much money on its prison system as it did on its universities. Since 1983, the California Department of Corrections has increased its staff by a huge 169%. . . . By contrast, California has decreased its higher education staff by 8.7%. The California Assembly Ways and Means Initial Review of the 1994/95 Budget states, "Corrections spending has grown more than twice as fast as total state spending. . . . This explosive growth has come at the expense of spending for other programs, primarily higher education."

Given that African Americans are significantly overrepresented in the jail and prison population—

> In 1991, African Americans constituted only 12.3% of the population nationwide, but 43.4% of the inmates in local jails, and 45.6% of the inmates in state prisons. (Rickford, 1997a, p. 173)

—they are undoubtedly the primary "beneficiaries" of the state's increased spending on prisons. But since spending on prisons comes at the expense of spending on schools, they are also the primary losers in this process. If one compares classrooms and school facilities in Palo Alto and East Palo Alto (Ravenswood), as I have, the latter are obviously far more poorly equipped in terms of buildings, books, computers, and other facilities than the former, and this difference alone must contribute to some of the differences in test scores between these school districts reported above.

Teacher pay, training, and collaboration

Teachers in highly successful school districts like Palo Alto tend to be better paid and to have received better training than teachers in less successful districts like East Palo Alto (Ravenswood). Interestingly enough, in the Evergreen Elementary School District in San Jose, California, which is only 17% White but "where schools consistently rack up academic awards and students outperform their peers across the county" (Suryaraman, 1997), teachers are paid an average of

$46,000 a year, among the highest in Santa Clara County. Additionally, Evergreen's teachers have high expectations for their students, are held and hold themselves to high standards of accountability, and spend Thursday afternoons attending training workshops and collaborating with each other on ways to teach better. This is surely a model worth emulating.

Outstanding (vs. mediocre) teachers

Apart from general factors like teacher training and pay, many school districts have one or more outstanding teachers. These include widely celebrated individuals like Pat Conroy (author of *The Water is Wide,* 1972, and the subject of the movie *Conrack*), Marva Collins (Collins & Tamarkin, 1982), Jaime Escalante (the real-life subject of the movie *Stand and Deliver*), and less well known figures like Oakland teacher Carrie Secret (see Miner, 1997) and East Palo Alto teacher Carl Daniels (see A. Rickford, 1998). Often, students who succeed against seemingly insurmountable odds have been influenced by star teachers like these. We need to study the strategies and philosophies that such teachers employ, while recognizing that we can never duplicate the whole package, and pass them on to other teachers. Actually, some of the factors listed below, like high expectations and the creation of challenging, engaging classrooms, are ones that almost invariably show up in the methodology of star teachers. Equally important is to identify and retrain or weed out the mediocre teachers who sometimes establish themselves securely in low-income, ethnic minority schools, where there is less competition for jobs. Based on recent classroom observations in California, I believe that poor teachers like these can have a stultifying effect on the educational and life opportunities of the children entrusted to their care.

Teacher expectations and pupils' performance

One of the factors that is well established in educational circles now is the powerful effect that teacher expectations can have on student performance (Tauber, 1997). Research studies indicate, however, that teachers tend to have lower expectations for African American students than for White students (Irvine, 1990). The effect can be particularly insidious for African American students who speak nonstandard or vernacular English because, as Williams (1976) showed, such students tend to be considered less promising or effective.

Stereotype vulnerability, self-esteem, and the need for challenge

A related factor is the "stereotype vulnerability" (Steele, 1992) that often develops among African American students, the low self-esteem, and the fear that they will inevitably succumb to the low expectations and prejudices of their teachers and fellow students. A common response to this on the part of African American students is "disidentification" with the academic enterprise and decreased effort (see Fordham & Ogbu, 1986). One solution to this stereotype vulnerability that Steele and others advocate is increased confidence building and challenge. For instance, Treisman's mathematics program for Black students at Berkeley (Treisman 1992) "recruits them to a challenging 'honors' workshop tied to their first calculus course. Building on their skills, the workshop gives difficult work" (Steele, 1992, p. 75). Students participating in this workshop quickly began to outperform their White and Asian counterparts. Similarly, Angela Rickford (1998) found that African American and other ethnic minority middle school students in East Palo Alto were more engaged and performed better when given a combination of ethnically congruent narratives and higher-order inferential and evaluative comprehension questions instead of the stultifying literal recall questions common in basal readers. Finally, Pollard and Ajirotutu (1997) showed that students at Martin Luther King Jr. elementary school in Milwaukee showed striking gains in reading, writing, and math after the school was designated an African immersion school in 1991. They argue that African-centered education might contribute more generally to increased cultural congruency and improved academic performance. At the same time, other factors like increased community and school district support were part of the success story at this elementary school.

Students' socioeconomic backgrounds

An obvious if little-understood factor in school success is the role of students' socioeconomic background. Students from higher socioeconomic backgrounds tend to do better than students from lower socioeconomic backgrounds, and because students of color are disproportionately represented among the latter,[9] the correlations between reading success and race discussed above must be partly attributed to socioeconomics, or class. At the same time, we should not make the currently popular mistake (of the many who favor replacing race-based with class-based affirmative action) of attributing *all* the variance to socioeconomics. For one thing, as the Draft Report of the University of California Outreach Task Force (1997) reveals, among California high school graduates who took the SAT in 1995, Black students whose families earned above $60,000 (the highest income bracket considered) scored lower (average of 810) than Latinos (904), Whites (995), and Asians (1050) in the same income bracket and lower than Whites in all income brackets, including the lowest, those below $20,000 (average of 899).[10] For another, we do not fully understand the factors that lie behind the correlations with class or race and their relative importance. Nutrition, parental involvement and support (a key element of the successful Comer schools [Comer, 1993]), provision of books and academic guidance within the home, orientation to schooling, racism—these and other factors are relevant, but they need further study. Lest people interpret the UC Task Force statistics as an invitation to revert to long-discredited genetic arguments, it should be noted that the task force itself suggests a number of explanatory factors for the grim correlations between SAT scores and race—"students' lives outside of school, their sense of the value of education, their self-confidence and esteem, . . . family support" (University of California Outreach Task Force, 1997)—but genetics is not one of them.

These are only some of the relevant nonlinguistic factors in African American students' school failure and success. It is important that linguists get involved in understanding and influencing these nonlinguistic factors as well as the linguistic ones if we want to see maximum yield from our involvement in school issues. I would also contend that if these other factors are held constant, a program that takes the linguistic background of AAVE speakers into account in teaching reading and the language arts is likely to be more successful than one that does not. As I show in sections 4 and 6, there is good evidence of this effect.

3. Improve teachers', students', and parents' attitudes and knowledge regarding AAVE.

The first and most popular response of linguists to public controversies about the role of AAVE and other vernacular dialects in education is to try to dispel the negative attitudes and expand the information that the public generally has about such vernaculars and about language in general. This was the essential strategy of Labov (1969) in the classic "Logic of Nonstandard English" article that he wrote in response to the allegations of educational psychologists that Black children were verbally deprived. A decade later, in the wake of the "Black English" trial of 1979 (see *The Ann Arbor Decision*, n.d.; Whiteman, 1980), the Ann Arbor School Board was directed by Judge Joiner, who had been strongly influenced by the testimony of linguists, to provide inservice training to help teachers learn more about AAVE and its educational consequences (Bailey, 1983). In the Oakland Ebonics controversy of late 1996 and early 1997, the systematic and complex nature of AAVE was repeatedly stressed by linguists—for instance in the Linguistic Society of America's January 1997 resolution on the Ebonics issue[11]—to counter the widespread public misperception that Ebonics is merely slang or lazy talk that should be eradicated. More recently, Wolfram and his colleagues (Wolfram, Adger, & Christian, 1999; Wolfram & Schilling-Estes, 1998) have emphasized the role that dialect awareness programs could play in increasing understanding of and appreciation for language variation in classrooms and communities. Their own dialect awareness programs in Baltimore, Maryland, and on Ocracoke Island, North Carolina—which reveal the grammatical and phonological regularity of local dialects as well as their distinctive lexicon and their historical origins—have been enthusiastically received by students, teachers, and community members and are widely regarded by sociolinguists as models for the field.

The deeper rationales for this educational response to public controversy (which we must be prepared to repeat over and over, as advertisers do—in the media, in classrooms, in public discussions, in private conversations) might include the following:

- Accurate diagnosis of a problem is essential to its adequate solution, and non-linguists' mistaken notions about what AAVE or other vernaculars are or what they reveal about children's cognitive abilities or scholarly potential are both unhelpful and harmful.

- Attitudes shape teacher expectations, which crucially affect student performance (Tauber, 1997), and negative attitudes rooted in ignorance of the rule-governed nature of vernaculars are likely to exacerbate the academic problems faced by their speakers.

- Students' self-esteem and interest in Standard English and the language arts tend to increase as they learn that their vernacular is a systematic and valid language form.[12]

But is it enough to attempt to improve public attitudes and information about AAVE, or should we also work to help AAVE speakers develop bidialectal competence in AAVE and SE? Kochman (1969) and Sledd (1972) both opposed the bidialectal program on various grounds, including the fact that it seemed hypocritical ("Your dialect is okay, but you need to learn SE"), that it placed the blame and responsibility for improvement on children rather than on the racism and ignorance of the larger society, that it wasted school time that could be used to develop children in more fundamental ways, and that it was ultimately likely to be unsuccessful either in developing solid competence in SE or in opening doors that were locked for reasons other than language. More recently, Lippi-Green (1997) has echoed similar sentiments about the "standard language myth" (she prefers the notion of "mainstream" U.S. English) and about the uncomfortable acceptance of language subordination and discrimination that the pursuit of teaching SE to vernacular speakers typically involves. But most linguists, while acknowledging these problems, still feel that for practical reasons (increased potential for success in schools and on the job) and because it is in line with the expressed self-interest of many African American students and parents, we need to improve access to SE or mainstream English even as we recognize the systematicity and complexity of the vernacular. Which brings us to the next point.

4. Improve the teaching of Standard English (SE).

Given that the goal of helping students master Standard English is shared by most detractors and aficionados of AAVE alike, it is evident that most of the media discussion about the Ebonics issue was about a non-issue. The real debate is, or should have been, about the *means* of teaching SE.

Immersion

For most commentators on the Ebonics issue, either implicitly or explicitly, the means of choice was and is immersion in the patterns, grammar, and spoken and written examples of SE without any reference to AAVE (considered either unnecessary, or likely to reinforce non-SE patterns, or both). One of the most explicit advocates of this approach is McWhorter (1997), who argues that

> we must make standard English a part of Black children's souls just as Black English is. This can only happen via immersion in standard English, to complement the immersion they have naturally had in Black English. (p. 4)

The most cogent rationale for advocating immersion as a means of improving the teaching of SE is evidence from second language teaching and learning that shows immersion to be one of the most effective ways of acquiring another language. But I have reservations about the effectiveness of this method for helping AAVE speakers acquire SE. For one thing, immersion seems to be more successful in the acquisition of a second language rather than a second dialect, where extensive overlaps in vocabulary, phonology, and grammar can cause speakers to miss subtle but significant differences between their own and the target variety. Secondly, where would SE immersion occur? The effect of exposure to SE via noninteractive media like radio and TV is apparently minimal. It is rather implausible to propose that SE be used exclusively in schools, including among AAVE-speaking friends. Immersion in SE in classrooms is already the method of choice in the overwhelming majority of U.S. schools. If it's so promising, why hasn't it produced better results?

Contrastive analysis

In a critique of the status quo with respect to English language instruction, Adger (1997) notes that "Programs to strengthen the standard English skills that schools require do not consistently point out predictable contrasts between standard and vernacular dialect features" (p. 2). Pointing out such contrasts so that students can identify and negotiate the differences between the vernacular and the standard is precisely the goal of contrastive analysis programs, which have been advocated for dialect speakers for more than 30 years (See, e.g., Feigenbaum, 1970).

The basic rationale for contrastive analysis as a means of teaching SE is that students who speak vernacular varieties of English—and their teachers—are typically not aware of the systematic differences between them. Le Page (1968) made this point in relation to the Creole Englishes of the Caribbean:

> The teachers *are* in most cases aware of the fact that the vernacular of the lower-middle class and working-class homes is different from the language they are supposed to use in the classroom, but they are not able to formulate in any methodical way where the differences lie or what they are due to. (p. 487)

Feigenbaum (1970), referring to vernaculars in the United States, made a similar observation:

> By comparing the standard English structure to be taught and the equivalent or close nonstandard structure, the student can see how they differ. Many students have a partial knowledge of standard English, that is, they can recognize and produce it but without accurate control. (p. 91)

The second rationale for contrastive analysis is that this method allows for increased efficiency in the classroom, as teachers can concentrate on the systematic areas of contrast with SE that cause difficulties for vernacular speakers rather than taking on the more daunting task of teaching all of English grammar. The SE features of contrast and potential difficulty (for instance, possessive -s for speakers of AAVE, who may write, for example, "the mother name"[13] instead of "the mother's name") can then be brought under conscious control through identification, translation, and other drills. Feigenbaum (1970) provides several examples of such drills, and there are hundreds of examples in the substantial handbook of the Proficiency in Standard English for Speakers of Black Language program, an SEP program that has been in use in California since the 1980s and is now in use in variant forms in over 300 schools, including several in Oakland. The 1996 Ebonics resolution was essentially a program to extend the SEP program within the Oakland Unified School District.

The third and perhaps most important rationale for using contrastive analysis to improve the teaching of SE is that where it has been systematically compared with other, more conventional methods, it has shown itself superior. Taylor (1989) reports, for instance, that African American students at Aurora University who were taught SE through an 11-week program of contrastive analysis showed a 59% decline in the intrusion of 10 Ebonics features in their SE writing, whereas a control group, taught by conventional methods over the same period, showed an 8.5% increase in the use of Ebonics features in their SE writing. Similarly, fifth and sixth graders in Kelli Harris-Wright's experimental program in DeKalb County, Georgia, who learn to switch consciously between "home language" and "school language" through contrastive analysis, show improved scores on the Iowa Test of Basic Skills each year, typically more so than the control groups of students who have been taught by other methods. (See chapter 3, this volume.)

One reservation that might be expressed about contrastive analysis programs for dialect speakers is that their potential or putative benefits are often extolled without the provision of empirical evidence. This is true, for instance, of Parker and Christ (1995), who report that they have used contrastive analysis successfully to help AAVE-speaking students in Tennessee and Chicago at the preschool, elementary, high school, and college levels develop competence in "Corporate English," but they provide no empirical evidence. This is also a problem with the SEP program in California, which has never been subjected to systematic, statewide evaluation (Yarborough & Flores, 1997), although such an evaluation is reportedly now being planned.

A second reservation is that the drills used in a contrastive analysis approach tend to be boring and repetitive, and if translation is not carried out in both directions, the message that can be conveyed is that the vernacular variety has no integrity or validity. In several contrastive analysis classrooms that I have observed in various parts of the country, translation is always from the vernacular to the standard, and it is sometimes referred to as "correction." In one particularly egregious case in California, in what was billed as an SEP classroom, the teacher put phrases and sentences on the board that were ungrammatical in AAVE and all known American vernaculars (e.g., "us coach" for "our coach") and asked students to correct them. However, these are not intrinsic weaknesses of contrastive analysis, and programs like the Language Development Program for African American Students in Los Angeles (LDPAAS),[14] which minimizes drills and makes extensive use of African American literature, show that they can be avoided.

A third, theoretical reservation one might express about contrastive analysis as a strategy for teaching Standard English as a second dialect is that it needs theoretical updating. In the field of second language acquisition, contrastive analysis was sharply discredited in the 1970s and 1980s because of its behaviorist orientations and because of the overly strong claim in Lado's (1957) Contrastive Analysis Hypothesis that virtually all the errors that second language learners make are attributable to the influence of their first language. Later analyses of errors made by people learning a second language revealed that no more than half, sometimes fewer, could be attributed to interference from the learner's first language (Ellis, 1994). However, contrastive analysis has been making a comeback under the heading of "language transfer" (Odlin, 1989), and its relevance to second language acquisition and teaching, reconceptualized in cognitive rather than behaviorist terms and with fuller attention to sociolinguistic competence (Danesi & DiPietro, 1991; Ellis, 1994), is now better established. Its usefulness in sharpening students' metalinguistic or cognitive awareness of language differences is also clear (Kenji Hakuta, personal communication, January 15, 1997).

The extent to which criticisms of contrastive analysis with respect to second language learning and teaching are relevant to second dialect learning and teaching is not yet clear, but contrastive analysis for Ebonics speakers should undoubtedly be supplemented with error analysis and with the insights and approaches that second language acquisition theory has developed since the 1960s. For instance, as far as I know, we do not have systematic scientific analyses of the extent to which the errors that Ebonics speakers make in speaking and writing SE reflect interference or transfer from Ebonics (in terms of which features are affected and how often). We have lots of anecdotal evidence that Ebonics is somehow relevant to these errors. But Labov (1995a) reported that an African American legal transcriber in Chicago made many errors with SE plural *s*-marking and few with verbal (third person singular) *s*-marking. This pattern is the opposite of what we would have predicted from the frequency with which these features occur in spontaneous Ebonics speech. We need more studies like this to validate the use of contrastive analysis as a tool for teaching SE to speakers of other English dialects.

These reservations should not be construed as reasons to deemphasize contrastive analysis. Contrastive analysis shows promise, and it should be used more often in teaching SE to AAVE speakers than it is now. At the same time, more research is needed to establish the efficacy of this method.

5. Improve the teaching of writing and speaking more generally.

Helping students increase their mastery of SE, which is the primary focus of many linguists and educators who are concerned about the education of AAVE speakers, is not enough. Teachers must also teach their students—including those who already speak SE—to read and read well (section 6) and help them improve their skills in writing and speaking. Teachers steeped in the African American oral tradition—for instance, Carrie Secret in the Oakland School District (see Miner 1997)—already provide opportunities for choral recitation and rhetorical expression that draw on traditional practices within the African American church and oral tradition. Hoover (1991) has proposed that we draw on those traditions to teach composition as well. Ball (1995) has suggested that distinctive community structures are also evident in the expository writing of African American students.

Smitherman (1994) makes the important point that the narrative-imaginative essays of African American college freshmen that were rated most highly by teachers were not necessarily those with the most consistent SE, but those that included features of what she calls the "African American discourse style." Certainly many of the most distinguished African American novelists, playwrights, and poets—including Maya Angelou, Claude Brown, Langston Hughes, Sonia

Sanchez, Alice Walker, and August Wilson—draw creatively on the African American vernacular as well as on SE, and several of them explicitly praise the vernacular.[15] African American schoolchildren should be allowed to draw creatively on AAVE in their written and spoken work too, to avoid the result of a stultifying concentration on SE that Le Page (1968) found in the Caribbean 30 years ago: "Many children are inhibited from any kind of creative expression at all; and the prizes go to the best mimics rather than the most talented" (p. 438).

In general, linguistically informed work dealing with the teaching of writing to AAVE speakers is not as voluminous as work dealing with the teaching of reading, but relevant references, in addition to those listed above, include Farr and Daniels (1986) and Wolfram, Adger, and Christian (1999).

6. Improve the teaching of reading.

It may seem curious to consider reading last, since most of the evidence in the first section dealt with failures in the teaching and learning of reading, and this critical skill is at the root of many students' success or failure in school, particularly at the elementary level. But last is by no means least, for while much more remains to be done, there has already been considerable linguistic scholarship on AAVE and reading. I summarize three primary lines of work: (a) Piestrup's (1973) research on the effects of teaching styles; (b) Labov's (1995b) linguistically informed suggestions for reading teachers; and (c) dialect readers.

Piestrup's (1973) research on the effects of teaching styles

Piestrup's important but little-known study (1973) of 208 African American first-grade children in Oakland, California, showed the typical relationship in which children who used more AAVE features had lower reading scores than other children. More interesting, however, was the relationship she demonstrated between alternative teaching styles—the way teachers responded to their pupils' language—and children's success in reading. The two extreme styles of the six she identified were the *Interrupting* and *Black Artful* styles. The Interrupting teachers "asked children to repeat words pronounced in [the vernacular] dialect many times and interpreted [vernacular] dialect pronunciations as reading errors" (p. iv). They had a chilling effect on the students' reading development, as reflected not only in reading scores lower than those of the Black Artful group, but also in the fact that some children "withdrew from participation in reading, speaking softly and as seldom as possible; others engaged in ritual insult and other forms of verbal play" (p. iv). By contrast, "teachers in the *Black Artful* group used rhythmic play in instruction and encouraged children to participate by listening to their responses. They attended to vocabulary differences of Black children and seemed to prevent structural conflict by teaching children to listen for standard English sound distinctions" (p. iv). Not only did children taught by this approach participate enthusiastically in reading, they also showed the highest reading scores, compared to children in the Interrupting and other groups. This study deserves replication by researchers and dissemination among teachers, to remind them that how they respond to vernacular-speaking students in the classroom crucially affects their students' success.

[margin annotation: results bad]

Labov's (1995b) linguistically informed suggestions for reading teachers

Labov (1995b), drawing on decades of research on AAVE, makes a number of linguistically informed suggestions for improving the teaching of reading to AAVE speakers. One of these is that teachers should "distinguish between mistakes in reading and differences in pronunciation." An AAVE speaker who reads aloud the words "I missed him" as "I miss him" has probably decoded the meaning of this Standard English sentence (i.e., "read" it) correctly, but he has reproduced it orally according to the pronunciation patterns of his vernacular, in which a consonant cluster like [st]—the final sounds in "missed"—is often simplified to [s]. Labov suggests that teachers give more attention to the ends of words, where AAVE pronunciation patterns have a greater modifying effect on SE words than they do at the beginnings. He also suggests that words be presented in contexts that preserve underlying forms: for instance, by using *testing* or *test of,* which favor retention of the final consonants, rather than *test* in isolation. These are sensible ideas, but as far as I know, no one has systematically implemented or evaluated them, so we have no empirical evidence of their effectiveness.

More recently, Labov and his colleagues at the University of Pennsylvania (Labov, Baker, Bullock, Ross, & Brown, 1998) have begun an empirical study of the kinds of decoding errors that AAVE speakers make in attempting to read the beginning, middle, and ending sounds of English words. The results so far are quite revealing and should prove especially useful to teachers.

Dialect readers

One approach that some have suggested (but note that neither Oakland nor Los Angeles is pursuing this approach) is that dialect speakers be introduced to reading with materials written in their native dialect and subsequently transitioned to reading in the standard or mainstream variety. Österberg (1961) and Bull (1990) reported striking successes in Sweden and Norway, respectively, showing in each case that dialect speakers taught by this method read better in the standard variety than dialect speakers taught through the standard variety alone.

The U.S. study most similar to these European studies was described by Simpkins and Simpkins (1981), who reported on an experiment involving the *Bridge* readers that they created in 1974 together with Grace Holt (Simpkins, Holt, & Simpkins, 1977). These readers, which were published by Houghton Mifflin in 1977, taught AAVE speakers to read by taking them through books written successively in AAVE, a transitional variety, and SE. The *Bridge* materials were tested over a 4-month period with 417 students in 21 classes throughout the United States (in Chicago, Illinois; Macon County, Alabama; Memphis, Tennessee; and Phoenix, Arizona). A control group of 123 students in six classes was taught using "regularly scheduled remedial reading" techniques. At the end of the 4-month period, students' scores on the Iowa Test of Basic Skills indicated that students taught by the *Bridge* method showed an average gain of "*6.2 months for four months of instruction*, compared to only an average gain *of 1.6 months* for students in their regularly scheduled classroom reading activities" (Simpkins & Simpkins, 1981, p. 238, emphasis in original). It should be noted, parenthetically, that the gain of only 1.6 months for 4 months of instruction that was evidenced by the control group is consistent with the evidence we saw in the first section that African American inner city children taught by regular methods tend to fall further and further behind mainstream norms each year they remain in school. It should also be noted, ruefully, that despite experimental demonstration of the success of the *Bridge* readers, some educators were so hostile to the presence of "dialect" in school materials that Houghton Mifflin halted publication, and this innovative and promising experiment ground to a halt. (See Rickford & Rickford, 1995, for further discussion.)

There have been other experiments with AAVE dialect readers in the United States, most of them successful, and there has been considerable discussion about the pros and cons of using them (see Baratz & Shuy, 1969; Fasold & Shuy, 1970; Laffey & Shuy, 1973; and Rickford & Rickford, 1995). The essential rationale for dialect readers is that they present AAVE speakers with the same initial task as that of SE speakers—learning to read (i.e., to extract meaning from print or writing)—without confronting them with the additional task of acquiring SE at the same time (Stewart, 1969). Dialect readers are almost invariably part of an overall program that includes a transition to reading and assessment in SE, so anxieties that SE will not be taught are unjustified. An additional point in favor of dialect readers is that they seem to work, both in increasing students' motivation and interest in reading and in improving their performance on comprehension and standardized reading tests.

One drawback to using dialect readers or teaching directly in the vernacular is that this tends to elicit knee-jerk negative reactions from parents and educators. Such a response can be minimized if those experimenting with dialect readers explain their rationale and display their commitment to parents and community members.[16] A second drawback is the fear that the use of dialect readers may involve (re)segregation of African American kids in special classes or special sections of classes. It is actually rather striking how many African American inner-city students are already in segregated classrooms. But even in integrated classrooms, it should be possible to introduce dialect readers to African American students as supplements to the regular reading materials and to SE speakers as part of a general consideration of language diversity in literature and real life.

A third and final reservation that was expressed in several studies in the early 1970s, including Melmed (1971) and Simons and Johnson (1974), is, as McWhorter (1997) put it: "Dialect readers were shown to have no effect whatsoever on African American students' reading scores" (p. 5). However, if one looks carefully at those studies, as I have, what is most striking is that they were all studies at one point in time of whether children decoded, discriminated, or comprehended better depending on whether the stimuli (words, sentences, short texts) were in AAVE or SE. The negative findings of these studies are certainly noteworthy and deserving of critical evaluation and replication, but one difference between these studies and the *Bridge* study (Simpkins & Simpkins, 1981) that I have already noted is that the *Bridge* study was conducted over a 4-month period, rather than at one point in time. That this may have been responsible for the differences in result is suggested by Simons and Johnson (1974),[17] one of the most substantive of the earlier studies reviewed by McWhorter:

> Another limitation of the present study concerns the length of the experiment and the number of reading texts employed. It may be the case that the treatment may have been too brief to show a difference in reading. (Simons & Johnson, 1974, p. 355)

Considerable work remains for linguists to do in re-examining, replicating and extending earlier research on the teaching of reading to AAVE speakers, whether our interest be in the study of decoding errors, the use of dialect readers, or the ways in which teachers should present material and respond to AAVE speakers in the classroom. As indicated in the second section, however, it is important for us to be aware of other aspects of the issue with which we have been less involved. In the case of reading, these include the use of phonics and phonemics versus whole language approaches (Chall, 1996), the importance of culturally relevant literature (Harris, 1995; Hornberger, 1985; A. Rickford, 1998), and the value of higher level inferential and evaluative comprehension questions rather than low-level recall questions (A. Rickford, 1998), particularly with students who have mastered the basic process of decoding. Linguists' research on reading has almost all been in the area of decoding, but the skill that all tests of

[handwritten margin note: treatment way too short]

21

reading involve is comprehension. While this critically involves decoding, it also involves much more.

Conclusion

In this overview I have tried to indicate why a conference and published proceedings on the language diversity of African American youth are necessary—the essential rationale being the devastating rates at which schools fail African American students—and I have outlined a number of strategies for dealing with this educational crisis. Although my focus was on the areas in which linguists have attempted to make a difference, such as the use of contrastive analysis in the teaching of SE and the use of dialect readers in the teaching of reading, I have tried to consider too the nonlinguistic issues, such as school facilities and teacher training, that also make a difference. I hope that more of us linguists will use our expertise and training to solve this and other practical crises in American life, and that we will do so with the interests of the children foremost in mind rather than our own intellectual predilections, differences, or biases. The stakes are too high for us to do otherwise.

Notes

1. Thanks to Carolyn Adger, Donna Christian, and Orlando Taylor for inviting me to give the opening address at this conference, and to my wife and intellectual companion, Angela Rickford, for helpful discussion of many of the relevant issues. Some portions of this paper draw on remarks in Rickford (1997b).

2. For example, from Angelou (1986), here is the opening verse of "The Pusher":

> He bad
> O he bad,
> He make a honky
> poot. Make a honky's
> blue eyes squint
> anus tight, when
> my man look in
> the light blue eyes.

And here is the closing verse of "The Thirteens":

> And you, you make me sorry
> You out here by yourself,
> I'd call you something dirty,
> But there just ain't nothing left,
> cept
> the thirteens. Right on.

3. This was evident in the title of the Oakland school board's controversial resolution, No 9697-0063, both in its original (December 18, 1996) and its amended (January 15, 1997) versions: "RESOLUTION . . . TO DEVISE A PROGRAM TO IMPROVE THE ENGLISH LANGUAGE ACQUISITION AND APPLICATION SKILLS OF AFRICAN AMERICAN STUDENTS."

4. Letter to Lukeman Literary Management, Ltd., New York.

5. Chances are that special interventions like extra encouragement, extra effort, extra time, and extra motivation on the part of parents, teachers, and students are involved in every success story.

6. Rev. Jackson subsequently visited the Oakland School District and reversed his position on the Ebonics issue, recognizing that "the teachers had not planned on teaching Ebonics but on using Ebonics to teach Standard English" (Watters, 1997, p. 1).

7. These data were drawn from the National Assessment of Educational Progress (NAEP). NAEP data from earlier years, dating back to 1971, indicate similar trends.

8. Note that these standardized tests are normed so that 50% of all students taking them are expected to score above the 50th percentile. It should also be noted that Hispanic students also showed declines between the elementary and high school levels—from 32% to 24.2% scoring above the norm—whereas Asian and Pacific Islander students showed increases (from 40.3% to 42.9%), as did Alaskan/Native American/Other students (from 37.4% to 53%).

9. In 1993, "the percentage of all US households whose earnings placed them below the poverty level was 15.1%; for Whites . . . 12.2%; for Hispanics, 30.6%; and for Blacks, 33.1%" (Rickford, 1997a, p. 174).

10. I am grateful to Gil Garcia of the U.S. Department of Education for sharing these data with me.

11. For the full text, see http://www.lsadc.org/web2/ebonicsfr.htm.

12. Fischer (1992, cited in Adger, 1997, p. 13) notes that "students [in a language awareness program for Caribbean English Creole speakers at Evanstown Township High School, Illinois] who clearly distinguish English as a separate language from Creole develop the motivation to tackle English language acquisition."

13. This example, drawn from the English composition of an African American college freshman at the University of Akron, is from Palacas (1998).

14. The LDPAAS, directed by Noma LeMoine, involves more than 90,000 African American students in the Los Angeles Unified School District. This program serves more students than does Oakland's program.

15. For instance, Alice Walker, in an interview in the March 21, 1981, issue of *The New Republic*, said: "The worst of all possible things that could happen would be to lose that language. There are certain things I cannot say without recourse to my language. . . . I know the standard English. I want to use it to help restore the other language, the lingua franca" (p. 27). And James Baldwin described AAVE in the *New York Times* (July 29, 1979) as "this passion, this skill, . . . this incredible music."

16. As Fischer (1992, p. 110) notes: "Many parents harbor the same prejudices against Creole as do their children, one of which is that Creole, while it may be fine to use at home and with friends, has no place in school. However, CAP [the Caribbean Academic Program in Evanston, Illinois] has taken the approach of explaining clearly and directly what we do and why, and parents have turned out to be very supportive."

17. It may turn out that the critical variable in the success of the *Bridge* readers was not their language, but the fact that they featured stories involving African American characters, situations, and themes that boosted motivation and interest. One replication might involve comparing the SE versions of the *Bridge* materials, which still include an African American focus, with other materials that lack this. However, AAVE is such an intrinsic part of the authenticity of the *Bridge* materials that it is difficult to know what the results of any such replication might mean; certainly A. Rickford (1998) suggests that the dialect in the dialog of some of her Black reading materials is an important element in their success.

References

Adger, C. T. (1997). *Issues and implications of English dialects for teaching English as a second language* (TESOL Professional Papers No. 3). Alexandria, VA: Teachers of English to Speakers of Other Languages.

Angelou, M. (1986). *Poems.* New York: Bantam.

The Ann Arbor decision: Memorandum opinion and order & the educational plan. (n.d.). Arlington, VA: Center for Applied Linguistics. (ERIC Document Reproduction Service No. ED 273 140)

Bailey, R. W. (1983). Education and the law: The King case in Ann Arbor. In J. W. Chambers, Jr. (Ed.), *Black English: Educational equity and the law* (pp. 1-28). Ann Arbor, MI: Karoma.

Ball, A. (1995). Text design patterns in the writing of urban African American students. *Urban Education, 30* (3), 253-289.

Baratz, J. C., & Shuy, R. W. (Eds.). (1969). *Teaching Black children to read.* Washington, DC: Center for Applied Linguistics.

Bull, T. (1990). Teaching school beginners to read and write in the vernacular. *Tromsø Linguistics in the Eighties, 11,* 69-84. Oslo, Norway: Novus.

Chall, J. S. (1996). *Learning to read : The great debate* (3rd ed.). Fort Worth: Harcourt Brace.

Collins, M., & Tamarkin, C. (1982). *The Marva Collins way: Returning to excellence in education.* Los Angeles: Jeremy Tarcher.

Comer, J. P. (1993). *School power : Implications of an intervention project* (2nd ed.). New York: Free Press.

Conroy, P. (1972). *The water is wide.* Boston: Houghton Mifflin.

Cose, E. (1997, January 13). Why Ebonics is irrelevant. *Newsweek,* p. 80.

Danesi, M., & Di Pietro, R. J. (1991). *Contrastive analysis for the second language classroom.* Toronto: Ontario Institute for Studies in Education.

Diringer, E., & Olszewski, L. (1996, December 21). Critics may not understand Oakland's plan: Goal is to teach black kids standard English. *San Francisco Chronicle,* p. A17.

Ebonics: Hearing before the Subcommittee on Labor, Health and Human Services, and Education, of the Senate Committee on Appropriations, 105th Cong., 1st Sess. (1997) (testimony of Michael Casserly).

Ellis, R. (1994). *The study of second language acquisition.* Oxford: Oxford University Press.

Farr, M., & Daniels, H. (1986). *Language diversity and writing instruction.* New York: ERIC Clearinghouse on Urban Education.

Fasold, R. W., & Shuy, R. W. (Eds.). (1970). *Teaching standard English in the inner city*. Washington, DC: Center for Applied Linguistics.

Feigenbaum, I. (1970). The use of nonstandard English in teaching standard: Contrast and comparison. In R. Fasold & R. W. Shuy (Eds.), *Teaching standard English in the inner city* (pp. 87-104). Washington, DC: Center for Applied Linguistics.

Fischer, K. (1992). Educating speakers of Caribbean English Creole in the United States. In J. Siegel (Ed.), *Pidgins, creoles, and nonstandard dialects in education* (Occasional Paper No. 12.) Canberra: Applied Linguistics Association of Australia.

Fordham, S., & Ogbu, J. U. (1986). Black students' school success: Coping with the burden of "acting White." *The Urban Review 18*(3), 176-206.

Freccia, N., & Lau, L. (1996, February). Sending kids to jail: Progress in California education. *Lift*, 1.02. Available: http://www.lifted.com/1.02/caleducation.html

Harris, V. J. (1995). Using African American literature in the classroom. In V. L. Gadsden & D. A. Wagner (Eds.), *Literacy among African-American youth: Issues in learning, teaching, and schooling* (pp. 229-59). Creskill, NJ: Hampton Press.

Hoover, M. R. (1991). Using the ethnography of African-American communications in teaching composition to bidialectal students. In M. E. McGroarty & C. J. Faltis (Eds.), *Languages in schools and society: Policy and pedagogy* (pp. 465-85). Berlin: Walter de Gruyter.

Hornberger, J. (1985). Literacy and Black children. In C. K. Brooks (Ed.), *Tapping potential: English and language arts for the Black learner* (pp. 280-285). Champaign-Urbana, IL: Black Caucus of the National Council of Teachers of English.

Hutchison, E. O. (1997). The fallacy of Ebonics. *The Black Scholar, 27*(1), 36-37.

Irvine, J. J. (1990). *Black students and school failure: Policies, practices, and prescriptions*. New York: Greenwood.

Kochman, T. (1969). Social factors in the consideration of teaching standard English. *The Florida FL Reporter, 7*(1), 87-88, 157.

Labov, W. (1969). The logic of nonstandard English. In J. E. Alatis (Ed.), *20th annual round table: Linguistics and the teaching of standard English to speakers of other languages or dialects* (pp. 1-38). (Monograph Series on Languages and Linguistics). Washington, DC: Georgetown University Press.

Labov, W. (1995a). Untitled paper presented at the Amherst Conference on African American English, University of Massachusetts, Amherst.

Labov, W. (1995b). Can reading failure be reversed: A linguistic approach to the question. In V. L. Gadsden & D. A. Wagner (Eds.) *Literacy among African-American youth: Issues in learning, teaching, and schooling* (pp. 39-68). Creskill, NJ: Hampton Press.

Labov, W., Baker, B., Bullock, S., Ross, L., & Brown, M. (1998). *A graphemic-phonemic analysis of the reading errors of inner city children* [Online]. Available: http://www.ling.upenn.edu/~labov/home.html

Lado, R. (1957). *Linguistics across cultures: Applied linguistics for language teachers*. Ann Arbor: The University of Michigan Press.

Laffey, J. L., & Shuy, R. (Eds.) (1973). *Language differences: Do they interfere?* Newark, DE: International Reading Association.

Le Page, R. B. (1968). Problems to be faced in the use of English as a medium of education in four West Indian territories. In J. A. Fishman, C. A. Ferguson, & J. Das Gupta (Eds.), *Language problems of developing nations* (pp. 431-43). New York: John Wiley and Sons.

Lewis, N. A. (1996, December 23). Black English isn't a second language, Jackson says. *New York Times*, p. B9.

Lippi-Green, R. (1997). *English with an accent: Language, ideology, and discrimination in the United States*. London and New York: Routledge.

McWhorter, J. H. (1997). Wasting energy on an illusion: Six months later. *The Black Scholar, 27*(2), 2-5.

Melmed, P. J. (1971). *Black English phonology: The question of reading interference* (Monographs of the Language Behavior Research Laboratory No. 1). Berkeley: University of California.

Miner, B. (1997). Embracing Ebonics and teaching standard English: An interview with Carrie Secret. *Rethinking Schools, 12*(1), 18-19, 34.

Odlin, T. (1989). *Language transfer: Cross-linguistic influence on language learning*. Cambridge: Cambridge University Press.

Österberg, T. (1961). *Bilingualism and the first school language—An educational problem illustrated by results from a Swedish language area*. Umeå, Sweden: Västernbottens Tryckeri AB.

Palacas, A. L. (1998, January). *Plurals in the English compositions of African American college freshmen.* Paper presented at the annual meeting of the Linguistic Society of America, New York.

Parker, H. H., & Crist, M. I. (1995). *Teaching minorities to play the corporate language game.* Columbia, SC: University of South Carolina, National Resource Center for the Freshman Year Experience and Students in Transition.

Piestrup, A. M. (1973). *Black dialect interference and accommodation of reading instruction in first grade* (Monographs of the Language Behavior Research Laboratory No. 4). Berkeley: University of California.

Pollard, D., & Ajirotutu, C. (1997). School restructuring in an African centered educational model. *Illinois Schools Journal, 75*(1) [Special issue: Focus on Afrocentricity and Afrocentric Education], 41-54.

Rickford, A. E. (1998). *I can fly: Teaching narratives and reading comprehension to African American and other ethnic minority students.* Lanham, MD: University Press of America.

Rickford, J. R. (1997a). Unequal partnership: Sociolinguistics and the African American speech community. *Language in Society, 26*(2), 161-197.

Rickford, J. R. (1997b, January). Ebonics and education: Lessons from the Caribbean, Europe and the USA. In C. Crawford (Chair), *What is the relationship of Ebonics to the education of Black Americans?* Symposium conducted at Medgar Evers College, New York.

Rickford, J. R., & Rickford, A. E. (1995). Dialect readers revisited. *Linguistics and Education, 7*(2), 107-128.

Simons, H. D., & Johnson, K. R. (1974). Black English syntax and reading interference. *Research in the Teaching of English, 8,* 339-358.

Simpkins, G. A., Holt, G., & Simpkins, C. (1977). *Bridge : A cross-cultural reading program.* Boston, MA: Houghton-Mifflin.

Simpkins, G. A., & Simpkins, C. (1981). Cross cultural approach to curriculum development. In G. Smitherman (Ed.), *Black English and the education of Black children and youth* (pp. 221-40). Detroit: Wayne State University, Center for Black Studies.

Sledd, J. (1972). Bidialectalism: The linguistics of White supremacy. In D.L. Shores (Ed.), *Contemporary English: Change and variation* (pp. 319-330). Philadelphia: J.B. Lippincott.

Smitherman, G. (1994). The blacker the berry, the sweeter the juice: African American student writers. In A. H. Dyson & C. Genishi (Eds.), *The need for story* (pp. 80-101). Champagne-Urbana, IL: National Council of Teachers of English.

Steele, C. (1992, April). Race and the schooling of black Americans. *The Atlantic Monthly, 269*(4), 68-78.

Stewart, W. A. (1969). On the use of Negro dialect in the teaching of reading. In J. C. Baratz & R. W. Shuy (Eds.), *Teaching Black children to read* (pp. 156-219). Washington, DC: Center for Applied Linguistics.

Suryaraman, M. (1997, January 10). School district achieves lots with little: Resourceful and focused, Evergreen shines despite "difficult" demographics. *San Jose Mercury News*, p. 1A.

Tauber, R. T. (1997). *Self-fulfilling prophecy: A practical guide to its use in education*. Westport, CT: Praeger.

Taylor, H. U. (1989). *Standard English, Black English, and bidialectalism*. New York: Peter Lang.

Treisman, U. (1992). Studying students studying calculus: A look at the lives of minority mathematics students in college. *College Mathematics Journal, 23*, 362-72.

University of California Outreach Task Force. (1997, July). *New directions for outreach: Report from the University of California Outreach Task Force to the University of California Board of Regents*.

Watters, B. (1997, January 2). Jackson gains new insight on Ebonics. *Chatham-Southeast Citizen*, p. 1.

Whiteman, M. F. (Ed.). (1980). *Reactions to Ann Arbor: Vernacular Black English and education*. Arlington, VA: Center for Applied Linguistics. (ERIC Document Reproduction Service No. ED 197 624)

Williams, F. (1976). *Explorations of the linguistic attitudes of teachers*. Rowley, MA: Newbury House.

Wolfram, W., Adger, C. T., & Christian, D. (1999). *Dialects in schools and communities*. Mahwah, NJ: Erlbaum.

Wolfram, W., & Schilling-Estes, N. (1998). *American English: Dialects and variation*. Oxford: Blackwell.

Yarborough, S., & Flores, L. (1997, January 19). Using Ebonics to teach standard English. *Long Beach Press-Telegram*, p. A1.

Chapter 2

The Language of African American Students in Classroom Discourse

Courtney B. Cazden

During the 1990s, the quality of classroom discourse has become prominent in discussions of school reform. This has happened for several converging reasons. According to two economists of education (Murnane & Levy, 1996), job success in the 21st century economy will require that high school graduates have not only competency in the 3Rs and with computers, but also "the ability to communicate effectively, both orally and in writing" (p. 32), and to work in teams with others from diverse backgrounds. With increasing diversity in our society and increasingly complex problems that citizens need to act together to solve, the abilities needed in the workplace are also necessary for effective participation in efforts toward a more democratic and just society. Closer to the traditional core of schooling, knowledge itself is now conceived less as inert information received from books and teachers and more as dynamic understanding constructed by students through intense discussion.

This new educational emphasis on communication calls for a dramatically different kind of classroom interaction that will promote such learning. Instead of the traditional pattern of classroom talk in which teachers ask test-like questions and students give short, test-like answers, teachers are being asked to lead discussions that stimulate and support "higher order thinking," and students are being asked to explain their reasoning, listen, learn from, and even argue with their peers. This shift in the demands of oral communication in the classroom is also reflected in the changing nature of high-stakes tests being introduced by districts or states. Instead of taking multiple choice tests, students are asked to construct answers to questions and write out explanations and arguments for them. Across the curriculum, classroom discourse has become more than the group context for individual student learning; it has become an essential and dynamic social process for accomplishing complex conceptual and communication goals.

At the same time, there has been a change in the way we think about the term *discourse* itself. It used to refer merely to any stretch of talk longer than a single sentence or, in the classroom, involving more than a single speaker. Gee (1996) offers what has become an influential distinction between that meaning, which he now calls "little d discourse," and what he calls "big D Discourse." This distinction calls our attention to what is entailed in the fluent enactment of any language pattern:

> A *Discourse* is a socially accepted association among ways of using language, other symbolic expressions, and "artifacts," of thinking, feeling, believing, valuing, and acting that can be used to identify oneself as a member of a socially meaningful group or "social network," or to signal (that one is playing) a socially meaningful "role."
> (Gee, 1996, p. 131)

Learning new ways with words thus entails taking on new interactional roles and the new identities they create and express.

It has always been the case that formal schooling requires forms of discourse from students that are different from the informal talk of home and street. But the more different these new forms are, the more attention we have to pay to helping all students learn to play their new roles. Educators from perspectives as different as those of Britain's Yanina Sheeran and Douglas Barnes (1991) and those of African Americans Lisa Delpit (1995) and Michele Foster (1997) urge teachers to be explicit with students about the ground rules for speaking and writing in these new roles. In other words, the cultural conventions of discourse itself have to be part of the new curriculum.

One way of thinking about Gee's little d/big D distinction with respect to Ebonics is to say that, in addition to the systems of formal features we call dialects, Discourse incorporates two aspects of language use long known to be important from a sociolinguistic perspective but often considered outside of linguistics proper: (1) "modes of discourse," so elegantly described and expressed in Smitherman's *Talkin and Testifyin* (1977/1986); and (2) language attitudes. This paper reports classroom research on these three topics: dialect learning, modes of discourse, and language attitudes.

Learning and Speaking Standard English

Pride of place belongs to Piestrup's (1973) research, *Black Dialect Interference and Accommodation of Reading Instruction in First Grade.* In her study of 14 first-grade classrooms, Piestrup found that where the use of Black dialect features during oral reading were negatively sanctioned by the teacher, children's use of those features actually increased over the year—perhaps in resistance to being placed in situations of conflict. In classrooms where teachers did not sanction students' use of Black dialect, the students decreased their use of Black dialect features during oral reading over the year and gained most in reading as measured by standardized tests. In Piestrup's interpretation, the latter group of teachers, whom she called "Black Artful" because of their use of rhythmic play in discourse, not only avoided structural conflicts over dialect differences (remember that Standard English is also a dialect) they also avoided functional conflicts over the children's attention and kept them focused on reading by using teaching strategies of playful firmness. Alone among all the studies reported here, Piestrup combined analyses of teachers' instructional strategies and interactional style with children's dialects and their academic achievement over the course of a school year. Conducted 25 years ago, it remains a model of useful research.

In the early 1980s, Lucas and Borders (1987, 1994) studied how students' use of dialect features changed with age. In their analysis of the incidence of nonstandard dialect features in a variety of events in kindergarten, fourth- and sixth-grade classrooms in a Washington, DC, school, Lucas and Borders found that whereas kindergarten children used such features in formal discussions with the teacher as well as in informal talk with peers, the fourth and sixth graders used virtually no nonstandard features in teacher-led recitations, even though such features still occurred in peer group talk. As Adger (1998) points out, however, "The fact that in teacher-led lessons children spoke far less than teachers, as is often the case, and that children's talk was functionally limited to responding, may have influenced the dialect patterning by constraining linguistic environments for dialect contrast" (p. 152). We need to replicate this study in the kind of nontraditional classroom discussions now being promoted across the curriculum.

Research more consonant with newer conceptions of classroom discourse that supports more complex conceptual understanding is Adger's own (1998) analysis of the language of African American vernacular speakers in five Baltimore elementary schools. She found that the students "regularly shifted toward the standard end of the dialect continuum within literacy events and in presentations where they adopted an authoritative footing [or stance] about the topic at hand" (p. 154). In other words, "speaking standard English meant speaking with academic authority" (Adger, 1998, p. 154).

Two other studies, carried out for other purposes, provide support for Adger's conclusion. One dates back to the late 1970s when peer teaching episodes from a classroom in San Diego were analyzed (Cazden, 1976). Mehan and Cazden called these episodes "instructional chains": Briefly, a child was taught a language arts task and then asked to teach that task to a peer. A report of the later videotape analysis of several of these chains contained this footnote about the speech of African American Greg and Mexican American Veronica in their role as tutors:

> Greg's careful, crisp, even exaggerated pronunciation of consonants in reading these sentences should be noted. That pronunciation makes it clear that his more casual, even slurred pronunciation at other times is indicative of style, *not* of dialect-based limitations on linguistic competence. Exactly the same exaggeratedly crisp pronunciation characterizes, even more surprisingly, the English spelling lesson Veronica teaches [in Spanish] to her bilingual peer. (Cazden, Cox, Dickinson, Steinberg, & Stone, 1979, p. 191; also summarized in Steinberg & Cazden, 1979)

A more recent study comes from one of the most visible current experiments in school reform: Brown and Campione's Fostering a Community of Learners in Oakland, California. Martha Rutherford (1995), a teacher researcher in the project, analyzed the oral and written discourse of one classroom of sixth graders in a science and literacy curriculum on the topic of endangered species. Prompted by the discussion of Adger's research at the conference that preceded this book, Rutherford went back to her dissertation and the data on which it was based. She found three contrasting discourse samples: a small group's initial planning discussion about which endangered species they wanted to research; their written proposal presented to the whole class; and their oral presentation on their research plan, also to the whole class. Extended excerpts from all three are presented in the appendix to this chapter, with Rutherford's annotations (personal communication, January 29, 1998). In the last two excerpts, the students are writing and speaking with authority about their plans, and the dialect and stylistic shifts from the language in the first excerpt are striking—shifts both toward Standard English and toward conventionally reasoned arguments.

It is important to note that Adger's hypothesis about the importance of the contextual variable of students' stance toward discourse content is not just an alternative name for the more familiar code-switching variable of change in addressee. In Rutherford's research, either stance or addressee could be the controlling variable, since teachers are included as addressees for only the more standardized versions; and in the instructional chains, the addressee is a peer with whom African American stylistic features would be expected. But Adger found that students generally used vernacular features in responding to the teacher but shifted toward standard features when they were asked to speak authoritatively. Thus it was stance and not addressee that co-occurred with the shift. Deborah Schiffrin (1997) explains the general point:

> Linguistic change and variation is influenced by people's positions not only in macrolevel global structures of society (and the access to power and privilege attendant with those positions), but also in microlevel, local structures in their communities. (p. 131)

African American students' macrolevel position in the larger society is an unfortunate given for each classroom teacher. But their microlevel positions in the classroom community are hugely influenced by the teacher's pedagogical practices.

The kinds of classroom discourse being recommended in current school reforms offer rich opportunities for students to adopt authoritative stances as they present, explain, and argue about knowledge. But what about the distribution of such opportunities? Are such discussions happening in the classrooms of African American students? And are they getting their fair share of classroom air time to discuss their ideas with their peers? Absent such opportunities, there is a danger that attempts to teach Standard English dialect features may leave African American students in the position of the students in lower tracked English classes in a Nova Scotia high school studied by John Willinsky:

> The enriched [higher track] academic students were assumed by their teachers to have an argument to make; they were expected to judge and to use language ably to defend those judgments. . . . [They] were to be trusted with both the language and the power of judgment. . . . The students at the general level had to prove their language was becoming more conventional, rather than their ideas more persuasive. . . . One group of students has had their attention directed to the avoidance of errors, an inducement to silence, while another was prompted to develop their voice, that they might be heard. (1988, pp. 135, 136)

We don't have to settle for only one objective. There is no inherent conflict for teachers between encouraging and, where necessary, teaching Standard English on the one hand, and involving students in the kinds of complex, extended discourse that demands judgment and reasons on the other hand; nor is there an inherent conflict for students, in Willinsky's terms, between avoidance of errors and developing their voice. The two objectives may be the explicit teaching focus of different activities in a total curriculum, as seems to be the case in Carrie Secret's (1997) classroom. But Adger's and Rutherford's research shows how they can also quite naturally be practiced together: a shift in conceptual and communicative function entraining a shift in codes.

Modes of Discourse

Smitherman (1977/1986) includes as "Black modes of discourse" two styles that have become the focus of classroom discourse research: narrative sequencing and call–response.

In a series of studies in California and the Boston area, Michaels and Cazden (summarized in Cazden, 1988) found striking differences in the narrative styles of White and African American children in one common primary grade speech event, Sharing Time. Whereas the White children tended to tell shorter narratives focused on one topic, the African American children, especially the girls, tended to tell longer and more complex narratives that fit Smitherman's description of "meandering away from the 'point' that takes the listener on episodic journeys and over tributary rhetorical routes" (1977/1986, p. 148). Analysis of the child-teacher interaction around the narratives showed that the White classroom teachers found the episodic narratives harder to understand and appreciate, and the African American narrators therefore did not get the kind of supportive interactions from which they could have expanded their narrative repertoire.

Aware of this academic research, two White primary school teacher researchers in the Boston area decided to conduct Sharing Time in their classrooms according to different rules, giving more responsibility for the event over to the children. In separate teacher research reports, Gallas (1992) and Griffin (1993) document the expanded narrative development of two African American children, Jiana and David. Both teachers attribute the children's development of clearer and more coherent narratives to the power of the child group—mixed in narrative styles as it was—in responding respectfully to Jiana's stories, and in participating dramatically in David's stories. After reading their reports, I would give the teachers more credit than they do themselves for their own role in listening carefully to the children and intervening in many ways to keep the mix of discourse styles in two-way stylistic balance.

In other words, these two teacher reports show that students can become bi-discoursal as well as bi-dialectal *if*—a big and important *if*—the teacher works constantly toward egalitarian relationships within the classroom community. Here, the influential microlevel variable is not the African American students' authoritative role or stance toward what they are talking about, as it is in Adger's study, but rather their equal-status interactions with their peers. In both cases, though in different ways, qualities of classroom group life assume importance for African American students' discourse development and academic achievement.

In several articles reporting her own research in successful classrooms of African American students at various grade levels and the research of others, Foster (1989, 1992, 1995) underlines the importance of "mutuality stemming from a group ethos":

> In all of the classrooms the teachers' attention is directed at the group. The interactions among the participants are marked by social equality, egalitarianism, and mutuality stemming from a group, not an individual ethos; cooperative, not competitive, behavior is reinforced in these classrooms. (1992, pp. 307-8)

Remember that even in Piestrup's early research, she attributed part of the Black Artful teachers' success to their playful firmness in reading group control.

Recently, a controversy has developed among educators, both African American and White, about the classroom usefulness of one group discourse mode: call–response. In 1988, composition theorist Anthony Petrosky visited schools in Sunflower County and Mound Bayou, Mississippi, because, despite extreme poverty, students there had tested well above state averages on a functional literacy examination. With the exception of one "impressive" teacher of writing, what he heard, in his interpretation, were choral responses to fill-in-the-blank teacher questions.

> It seems possible that the language of this rural black culture (at least as it is represented by the call-and-response tradition) has been subverted to the language of the "basic skills" technology, perhaps simply because the fit of the call and response to that technology is so good, . . . a technology of recitation and drill in manners that closely mimic testing situations. (Petrosky, 1990, pp. 65, 69)

Petrosky goes on to question the belief that may underlie this practice—that basic skills have to precede higher order literacies—and he worries that school success in one ill-prepares students for the other. "Do we, for example," he asks, "learn the Bill of Rights by memorizing it or by, say, writing interpretive essays about it?" (1990, p. 70).

A teacher researcher in the Mississippi Delta read Petrosky's report as part of a literature review, *Between a Rock and a Hard Place: African Americans and Standard English* (Moore, 1996). In her final section, "Beyond Methodology: Culturally Engaged Instruction," Moore's first positive example of African American discourse style in schools comes from Petrosky's report. Without mentioning his concerns, she reports Petrosky's observation that, in her words, "the teach-

Is memorization better than interpretation? Or

ers at these two [successful] schools (the majority of whom were Black) relied heavily on a 'call-and-response' type of classroom recitation" (p. 30). So we have one pattern of classroom discourse that is interpreted very differently by White university researcher Petrosky and African American teacher Moore.

How should we understand these contrasting positions? In Gee's terms, is call–response standing for larger Discourse complexes in these two educators' minds? Is it standing for the limitations of individual rote learning and the kinds of knowledge that can be expressed in choral responses for Petrosky, while standing for a culturally valued emphasis on memorization, performance, and group solidarity for Moore? Consider language use in any classroom as expressing and accomplishing three large categories of universal language macro-functions: the referential construction and communication of ideas, the establishment and maintenance of social relationships, and the expression of participants' social identities and attitudes (Cazden, 1988). In his critique, does Petrosky have in mind only the referential language function, while Moore recognizes the importance of the relational and identity functions as well?

What are useful roles for a secular classroom adaptation of this call–response discourse mode that derives originally from sacred tradition? Reading Petrosky's examples, I was reminded of my own observations in Mississippi Delta classrooms during the 1993-1994 school year, when I joined a biracial team observing the implementation of Robert Moses's Algebra Project (Moses, Kamii, Swap, & Howard, 1989). The Algebra Project (AP) curriculum is designed to build students' competence and confidence in understanding math and in speaking up to explain and defend their answers, and we saw elegant examples of just that. My observational notes from two classrooms also include brief interludes of interactions whose participant structure fits Petrosky's examples. In one class, an African American teacher started her class like this:

T.   The Algebra Project teaches you to what?
Ss (in unison) Think!
T.   It teaches you to think how?
Ss (in unison) Critically!

Then she shifted smoothly to assigning small group tasks and later probing the students' reports back to the whole group. In another class, a White teacher elicited a choral response for the definition of a prime number; then during team competition in an activity called the "winding game"—using base 12, so that, for example, 50 = 4 w[inds] + 2—someone started to laugh at a peer's mistake.

T.   Since when in this class do we *ever* fry anyone over a mistake? (Silence)
T.   Does the winder get points?
Ss   (in unison) Nooo.
T.   Is the winder learning from his mistake?
Ss   (in unison) Yeees.

In both classrooms, these short interludes seemed to express and solidify a communal commitment to AP norms of learning, speaking, and relating. In the first classroom, they also elicited a memorized definition, a useful function if the choral response serves as a reminder of deeper understanding gained through nonformulaic discussion at another time.

Finally, are both Petrovsky and I misinterpreting the call-response tradition by applying this label to our observations? Smitherman (1977/1986, pp. 104-124) emphasizes spontaneous, complementary variation rather than unison memorizations in listeners' "talking back" to a speaker, and that is also what Shirley Brice Heath remembers from her southern childhood (personal communication, April, 98). What might more authentic classroom adaptations of this discourse mode sound like and accomplish? Foster's current research on a professional development program for teachers of African American students in the San Francisco Bay area may give us better answers to this cluster of important questions (personal communication, January, 1998).

The Importance of Language Attitudes

In this last section, we will look at five reports that document the power of attitudes—those of teachers and students, both White and Black—toward talking about, as well as using, standard and nonstandard varieties of English. All five are by teachers, two from college and three from public schools. The first is poet and essayist June

Jordan's (1985) essay, "Nobody mean more to me than you and the future life of Willie Jordan."

In 1984, Jordan was professor of English at State University of New York, Stonybrook, teaching a new course called "In search of the invisible Black woman" to a large class of Black women and men and five or six White students. When she assigned *The Color Purple* and initiated discussion of the first 40 pages, the students sat silently, studying their hands or the floor. "The tense, resistant feeling in the room fairly astounded me" (Jordan, 1985, p. 124). Finally, someone spoke up: "Why she have them talk so funny. It don't sound right" (p. 125). Jordan reports: "At this, several students dumped on the book. Just about unanimously, their criticisms targeted the language" (p. 125). Needless to say, Jordan was up to the challenge, and the class worked on understanding and valuing "three qualities of Black English—the presence of life, voice, and clarity—that testify to a distinctive Black value system that we became excited about and self-consciously tried to maintain" (p. 129).

Then an intellectual crisis arose for the class when the brother of one student, Willie Jordan (no relation to the teacher), was killed by the police. The class wrote messages in Black English to Willie, his family, and the police, then decided to send all these messages with an introductory paragraph to *Newsday*. When it came to deciding whether the opening paragraph should be written in Black English or Standard English, Jordan says, "I have seldom been privy to a discussion with so much heart at the dead heat of it" (Jordan, 1985, p. 135).

A different kind of resistance and heat confronted cognitive psychologist Linda Flower when she was working as an adult leader with college student mentors and teenage writers in a 9-week collaboration between the University of Pittsburgh and a local community literacy center (CLC). The following is from her reflective report, "Negotiating the Meaning of Difference."

> The language of the CLC is the language of a border zone where the discourses of problem solving, writing strategies, and policy argument are trying to work hand in hand with the performative discourse of African American community making, the prophetic tradition of Black struggle, and the street talk of urban teenagers. (Flower, 1996, p. 48)

At one point, the teenagers had spent 8 weeks developing a 12-page document they called "Street Life: Dealing with Violence and Risk in our Community," which they were to use in a public conversation to argue for social action on issues affecting their lives. During the evolution of the document, Flower "wanted to remind writers that they would need to make decisions about when to use standard Written English (SWE) and when to use Black English (BE), given their audience of both peers and policy makers" (p. 53). Although she intended only to initiate discussion of the strategic decision about which code to use, what erupted was heated confusion over not just the use but the very existence of Black English. It is this "heated confusion" that Flower spends 30 self-reflective pages trying to understand. In the end she concludes,

> It soon became apparent that the real struggle here was not how to transmit my understanding [about the linguistic status of Black Dialect as a rule-governed system in its own right] but how to transform it. . . . [That transformation] can involve decided shifts in power relations when the scholarly discourse of linguistic description gives up its seat of authority to the political discourse of social consequences and the compelling truth of experience. (1996, p. 84)

We should not be surprised that attitudes toward language variation can be so powerful. Together, these two reports raise a question about what, beyond linguistic knowledge, needs to be included in a curriculum about language variation, especially for older students.

In the excellent special issue of *Rethinking Schools* on the Ebonics debate, perhaps the single most important article is the interview with Oakland (CA) fifth-grade teacher Carrie Secret (Secret, 1997). The title of the interview expresses the essence of her work: "Embracing Ebonics and Teaching Standard English." Secret has many ways of working explicitly with the contrasting codes she labels for the children as Ebonics and English, calling their attention to contrasts in both features and situations. But it would be an unfortunate reduction of her total curriculum to remember and transfer only that component. Equally important are her strategies for teaching high-level literacy and "the content language of each area of the curriculum." Equally important are her many ways of "embracing Ebonics"—for example, by having the children memorize poems by African American poets who write in both styles. With all that and more, it is not surprising that even the parents of her fifth graders have lost their shame about their language. Ladson-Billings' (1994) stories (her term) about eight successful elementary teachers of African American children, five Black and three White, include many of Secret's strategies, although only one story (pp. 83-84) mentions language variation.

For Mississippi high school teacher Moore, including explicit attention to both codes in her curriculum seems to be more difficult than it is for elementary school teacher Secret. Moore's literature review begins with a statement from Asa Hilliard about the need to understand issues of language and the education of African American children in "the history of the role and dynamics of language in the context of oppression" (Hilliard, 1983, p. 24). Sadly, Moore sees "that same conflict torment another generation of African Americans."

> As an African American woman teaching at a rural all-Black high school in the Mississippi Delta, I enjoy a genuine fellowship with my students, many of whom I work with outside of school. Nevertheless, whenever I begin teaching grammar or usage, my students put up a fearful, sometimes hostile, resistance. Yet, in my class surveys and course evaluations, the students and their parents have consistently asked that I teach *more* grammar. At first, I tried to account for these contradictions with various excuses. . . . Still, the tension and the fear are real. Looking back, I realize I shared their uneasiness with the topics but felt it was my duty to help them become proficient in "standard" usage. The truth is teaching English/language arts involves more complex questions and unresolved issues than many of us either realize or admit. (Moore, 1996, p. 2)

Moore concludes that "the success (or failure) of particular teaching methods has more to do with the cultural and political factors involved than with any particular pedagogical formula" (1996, p. 34).

In this small sample of teacher reports, the more negative—or at least ambivalent—attitudes toward explicit discussions of dialect differences are expressed by older students in high school and college (Moore, Flower, and Jordan, as contrasted with Secret and Ladson-Billings). Perhaps for them, attention to discourse conventions is not enough, and another component needs to be included in the curriculum: what Moore calls "cultural and political factors" and Flower speaks of as "the political discourse of social consequences and the compelling truth of experience."

High school teacher Linda Christensen in Portland, Oregon, makes the political factor explicit to her students. In a report on her own teaching, "Whose Standard? Teaching Standard English," Christensen (1989-90) describes the many activities through which she, like Carrie Secret, teaches Standard English. Then her final section, "Learning the 'Standard' Without Humiliation," begins, "But the lessons can't stop there." She goes on:

> Asking my students to memorize the rules without asking who makes the rules, who enforces the rules, who benefits from the rules, who loses from the rules, who uses the rules to keep some in and some out, legitimates a social system that devalues my students' knowledge and language. . . . It took me years to undo what Mrs. Delaney [a teacher who corrected her own white working class language] did to me. . . . For too long, I felt inferior when I spoke. I knew the voice of my childhood crept out, and I confused that with ignorance. It wasn't. I just didn't belong to the group who made the rules. I was an outsider, a foreigner in their world. My students won't be. (1989-1990, p. 145)

Especially for older students, a curriculum of cultural critique may be as important as a curriculum of cultural conventions.

Conclusions

The increased importance of discourse in school reform teaching and testing brings both positive and negative possibilities for greater educational equity for African American students. On the positive side, if students' oral language abilities are considered resources for learning additional ways with words, their gains can be considerable. Negatively, if those new ways with words are required in high stakes assessment, differential opportunities to learn, communicatively as well as conceptually, will be even more damaging.

In a reflection on research on the language of African American students of the 1960s and 1970s, educational linguist Arnetha Ball writes:

This prior research succeeded in providing a more complex and more complete profile of the linguistic practices of diverse populations. However, it did little to influence classroom practice. In spite of considerable efforts of this [linguistic] research community over the past twenty years, recent research indicates that the linguistically-based research of the 1960s and 1970s was never translated into widespread application within most traditional classroom settings. (personal communication, 1997)

With the benefit of the research reported here—research by teachers as well as outside observers and analysts—we should be able to do a better job.

References

Adger, C. T. (1998). Register shifting with dialect resources in instructional discourse. In S. B. Hoyle & C. T. Adger (Eds.), *Kids talk: Strategic language use in later childhood* (pp. 151-169). New York: Oxford University Press.

Cazden, C. B. (1976). How knowledge about language helps the classroom teacher—Or does it? A personal account. *The Urban Review, 76*(9), 74-90. (Reprinted in *Whole language plus: Essays on literacy in the United States and New Zealand* [chapter 3], by C. B. Cazden, Ed., 1992, New York: Teachers College Press)

Cazden, C. B. (1988). *Classroom discourse.* Portsmouth, NH: Heinemann.

Cazden, C. B., Cox, M., Dickinson, D., Steinberg, Z., & Stone, C. (1979). "You all gonna hafta listen": Peer teaching in a primary classroom. In W.A.Collins (Ed.), *Children's language and communication: The Minnesota Symposia on Child Psychology, Vol. 2* (pp. 183-231). Hillsdale, NJ: Erlbaum.

Christensen, L. (1990). Whose standard? Teaching standard English. *Rethinking Schools, 4*(2), 142-145. (Reprinted from *English Journal,* 1990, *79*(2), pp. 36-40) (Reprinted in *Rethinking schools: An agenda for change*, pp. 128-135, by D. Levine et al., Eds., 1995, New York: New Press)

Delpit, L. (1995). *Other people's children: Cultural conflict in the classroom.* New York: New Press.

Flower, L. (1996). Negotiating the meaning of difference. *Written Communication, 13*, 44-92.

Foster, M. (1989)."It's cookin' now": A performance analysis of the speech events of a Black teacher in an urban community college. *Language in Society, 18*, 1-29.

Foster, M. (1992). Sociolinguistics and the African-American community: Implications for literacy. *Theory into Practice, 31*, 303-311.

Foster, M. (1995). Talking that talk: The language of control, curriculum, and critique. *Linguistics and Education, 7*, 129-150.

Foster, M. (1997). What I learned in Catholic school. In C.P. Casanave & S. R. Schecter (Eds.), *On becoming a language educator: Personal essays on professional development* (pp. 19-27). Hillsdale, NJ: Erlbaum.

Gallas, K. (1992). When the children take the chair: A study of Sharing Time in a primary classroom. *Language Arts, 69*, 172-182. (Reprinted in *The languages of learning: How children talk, write, dance, draw, and sing their understanding of the world* [chapter 2], by K. Gallas, 1994, New York: Teachers College Press)

Gee, J. P. (1996). *Social linguistics and literacies: Ideology in discourses* (2nd ed.). Bristol, PA: Taylor & Francis.

Griffin, S. (1993). "I need people": Storytelling in a second-grade classroom (The Literacies Institute Technical Report No. 11). Newton, MA: Educational Development Center.

Hilliard, A. G. (1983). Psychological factors associated with language in the education of the African American child. *Journal of Negro Education, 52*(1), 24-34.

Jordan, J. (1985). Nobody mean more to me than you and the future life of Willie Jordan. In *On call: Political essays* (pp. 123-139). Boston: South End Press.

Ladson-Billings, G. (1994). *The dreamkeepers: Successful teachers of African American children.* San Francisco: Jossey-Bass.

Lucas, C., & Borders, D. (1987). Language diversity and classroom discourse. *American Educational Research Journal, 24*, 119-141.

Lucas, C., & Borders, D.G. (1994). *Linguistic diversity and classroom discourse.* Norwood, NJ: Ablex.

Moore, R. (1996). *Between a rock and a hard place: African Americans and standard English.* (ERIC Document Reproduction Service No. ED 402 593)

Moses, R. P., Kamii, M., Swap, S. J., & Howard, J. (1989). The Algebra Project: Organizing in the spirit of Ella. *Harvard Educational Review, 59*(4), 27-47.

Murnane, R. J., & Levy, F. (1996). *Teaching the new basic skills: Principles for educating children to thrive in a changing economy.* New York: Free Press.

Petrosky, A. (1990). Rural poverty and literacy in the Mississippi Delta: Dilemmas, paradoxes, and conundrums. In A. A. Lunsford et al. (Eds.), *The right to literacy.* New York: Modern Language Association.

Piestrup, A. M. (1973). *Black dialect interference and accommodation of reading instruction in first grade.* Berkeley, CA: University of California, Language–Behavior Research Laboratory.

Rutherford, M. (1995). *"We can't fight with our fists. Words are our power":* *Teaching children in the middle school years learning to write academic prose.* Unpublished doctoral dissertation, University of California, Berkeley.

Schiffrin, D. (1997). Stories in answer to questions in research interviews. *Journal of Narrative and Life History, 7*(1-4), 129-137.

Secret, C. (1997). Embracing Ebonics and teaching standard English: An interview with Oakland teacher Carrie Secret. *Rethinking Schools, 12*(1), 18-19, 34. (Reprinted in *The real Ebonics debate: Power, language and the education of African-American children,* by T. Perry & L. Delpit, Eds., 1998, Boston: Beacon Press & Rethinking Schools)

Sheeran, Y., & Barnes, D. (1991). *School writing: Discovering the ground rules.* Philadelphia: Open University Press.

Smitherman, G. (1986). *Talkin and testifyin: The language of Black America.* Detroit: Wayne University Press. (Original work published 1977)

Steinberg, Z. D., & Cazden, C. B. (1979). Children as teachers—of peers and ourselves. *Theory into Practice, 18,* 258-266.

Willinsky, J. (1988). *The well-tempered tongue: The politics of standard English in the high school.* New York: Teachers College Press.

Appendix[1]

The students in this group are Numbala, Terra J, and Jerry, African Americans; and Daniel and Flora, Mexican Americans.

Taken together, these three examples show that the choice of what kind of language to use in a given circumstance was deliberate, motivated by both audience and purpose.

First excerpt: Small group planning discussion

The students needed to pick as a research topic some endangered species. Choices were limited by available resources. The group was told they would be well served to have three possibilities in case they didn't get their first choice. After deciding on a topic, the group submitted a proposal to a review board of teachers. Proposals receiving the most points were awarded their first choice. (This was meant to be like writing a proposal for a funding agency.)

Although the students knew that when they came back to the whole class, they would have to support their choice by presenting some "conventional" reasons why they should get a certain topic, such reasons played no part in their small group discussion. If, in this situation, some member of the group had used "academic speech," that person would not have been persuasive.

Numbala:	Primates! Primates! Primates!
Terra J:	Are you talkin' to me? Stop touchin' me!
Numbala:	Primates! Primates!
Daniel:	They are dangerous.
Jerry:	Gorillas ain't dangerous.
Terra J:	I love all monkeys, even the ugly ones . . . baboons . . .
Daniel:	She loves all of the monkeys!
Terra J:	I did a report on monkeys in the fourth grade. I got an E on it.
Jerry:	Bears.
Numbala:	Look here . . . we doin' primates. I want primates.
Jerry:	No, we ain't, we doin' bears.
Terra J:	You ain't nobody. I 'bout to get mad at you.
Numbala:	Hey, hey, hey, look you want sea otters instead of primates?
Daniel:	No, I don't . . .

Terra J:	We ain't getting no big cats. Everybody in here want big cats.
Numbala:	Bears is first, primates is second, and wildcats.
Terra J:	Primates is first, bears is second, and wildcats last.
Numbala:	That's just 'cause you like those little, stupid chimpanzees.
Daniel:	Big cats . . .
Terra J:	Jerry, go sit down, that's not what we suppose to be doing!
Jerry:	So.
Terra J:	You sit down before you make our group look bad 'cause of your stupid . . . little . . . why you act like little children?
Numbala:	'Cause we feel like it sometimes.
Terra J:	Why you actin' like that?
Jerry:	'Cause we want to.
Numbala:	And like you're not immature!
Jerry:	I ain't goofin' around.
Terra J:	You not goofin' around? Lord bless us all.
Numbala:	Oh . . . God! You so crazy. You know you lyin'.
Terra J:	I need to work with a much more mature . . . serious group.

Second excerpt: Written presentation the same day

After the discussion, the group wrote the following short piece, which Terra J presented to the whole class. This piece is well supported with conventional reasons why they should have their topic, primates. These two exchanges happening in such close proximity shows how facile these students were in their use of different language styles.

Primates are very interesting to learn about especially when you compare them to humans. We feel that learning about primates will be a very good experience and especially since there are so many of them, we would like to learn about their foods how they protect and do they camouflage, we came up with a lot of questions about primates such as are they omnivores, what other foods do they eat, how many different primates are there in the world, we also wanted to compare chimpanzees to gorillas because gorillas are

50

much bigger than chimpanzees and they might eat the same foods who knows? So we feel that this will be an interesting topic to study and might do us some good in life.

Third excerpt: Oral presentation the next day

The group presented their research plan to the whole class. This oral presentation is also supported by conventional reasons.

Numbala: We talked it over and um . . . then we voted on what we would like to do. We . . . um . . . didn't argue about it we just decided. Some people wanted to vote on what everybody would do. We wrote up our arguments and some people said the same thing.

Terra J: Do you want us to read our arguments?

Teacher A: Yes.

Terra J: I have chose reproduction 'cause learning about how a new child is brought into life is important. I learned about human reproduction and I'm sure the primate is the closest to the human. I want to know how much do baby primates weigh . . . etc. . . . . What I learn I will be able to carry into the future and teach other people and interest them in animal research.

Numbala: Since there are six topics some of us will get two topics. I wanted defense mechanisms 'cause I wanted to learn what apes and primates do and how they protect themselves and how they use weapons and when they use them the most.

Daniel: Mine is habitats. I wanted habitats 'cause I wanted to know more about primates' habitats—where they make their habitat—how they make their habitat and what kind of things they use to make it and if they use things like humans to make their habitat.

Flora: I picked food and water 'cause animals can't survive without them. Food or water is important 'cause animals, if animals don't have water and drink water they won't survive.

Jerry: I want defense mechanisms because I want to learn how it defends itself in battle. I want to know how an ape uses its strength to rip a man in half.

Note

1. From Rutherford, M. (1995; personal communication, 1998) with annotations by Rutherford.

Chapter 3

Enhancing Bidialectalism in Urban African American Students[1]

Kelli Harris-Wright

Speaking and listening are routine in classrooms. Teachers speak; students listen. Students speak and teachers listen, comment, and ask and answer questions. Teachers generally control the flow of communication in classrooms by exercising authority (Delpit, 1995), but they do not fully control the ways in which students speak. The way a student communicates a response surely influences the teacher's perception of its appropriateness. Thus students' communication skills bear on academic achievement. Teachers' judgements of students' participation are more positive when students communicate ideas that are directly related to the topic, state those ideas articulately and primarily in Standard English form, use voice tones and intonation patterns that suggest confidence and knowledge of the implicit social demands of the situation, and display nonverbal behaviors that enhance communication (Cazden, 1988). In other words, students whose communication skills match teachers' culturally based expectations are more likely to be perceived as providing appropriate responses.

Teachers expect students to participate in classroom discourse using what may be termed a "literate style," in which a topic is introduced, discussion sustained, and points summarized in a fairly linear progression. Often the communicative situation demands that a student listen and wait to be recognized by the teacher or group leader before talking. At other times, instructional arrangements may require students to communicate together and report back to the teacher.

For most mainstream students, following the implicit rules for communication at school is easy. For many African American students and other culturally and linguistically diverse students, the patterns of communication inherent in school success may be unfamiliar, because these rules and communicative routines have not been part of their previous socio-cultural experience (Saravia-Shore & Garcia, 1995). If they are unaware of how African American students' communication skills may affect their classroom performance, teachers may misanalyze students' talk and provide feedback to them and to other educators based on their misanalysis (Crago, Eriks-Brophy, McAlpine, & Pesco, 1997). When African American students do not realize the critical relationship between classroom communication patterns and teachers' judgments of their ability to understand or relate to others, and when they are unable to communicate in ways that match the expectations of school and workplace, they may fall deeply into the chasm of underachievement (Perry & Delpit, 1997). To address this barrier to student success, students and teachers need to learn about each others' communicative patterns and expectations. To facilitate this metalinguistic task, teachers must assume responsibility for creating an environment of mutual respect in which this learning can occur.

Educators seem more reluctant to acknowledge and learn about the historical and cultural bases of the language and communicative systems of African American students than about those of speakers of languages other than English. Many educators either do not know or do not care to know the details of African American Vernacular English, and they have not been able to plan appropriate literacy development strategies for African American vernacular speakers. As a result, disproportionate numbers of African American vernacular-speaking students continue to be placed in special education and remedial programs. Teachers need explicit, detailed, and appropriate knowledge about African American students' communicative systems so that they can adopt effective instructional practices that support their language development. This is not to suggest that African American vernacular speakers need only to develop a literate discourse style and Standard English forms in order to be successful in school. Much more is needed, but the lack of explicit instruction in these domains will surely sabotage other efforts.

Traditional Approaches

Traditionally, African American vernacular speakers have been taught mainstream English through two basic approaches: (1) eradication of vernacular features and (2) no intervention at all. Unfortunately, neither has been particularly effective in producing students who can, by choice, use Standard English written and oral communication patterns effectively. Eradication approaches have taught the rules of Standard English as a replacement dialect, attempting to wipe out the vernacular grammatical and phonological features and other aspects of language learned in the home. In the no-intervention approach, educators have been reluctant to expect Standard English use by African American vernacular speakers, because they recognize that the vernacular is a product of the students' culture. Rather than offending students through poorly informed feedback, teachers say nothing that could provoke a change in language patterns to include a standard literate style.

The Bidialectal Program

For more than 10 years, the DeKalb County School System in Georgia has been operating a program to teach mainstream English and school communication skills to students without devaluing the language skills that they learn at home (Harris-Wright, 1987). The program is made available through Title I, and it is coordinated with the language arts and reading programs. The bidialectal program recognizes the need for all students to be able to function in the common culture and supports the efforts of culturally and linguistically diverse populations to preserve their identities (Adler, 1987, 1993). Students in the program learn that communication is sensitive to the relationship of the speakers, the purpose for speaking, and the context for communicating. To accommodate changes in these factors, two ways of communicating must become routine for speakers of vernacular dialects.

Students are given unpressured and uninterrupted opportunities to listen to the sounds and patterns of Standard English as used in authentic contexts. They have guided and independent practice in Standard English communication skills. These activities occur in environments that do not require African American vernacular speakers to shed their identities as a prerequisite for learning Standard English.

The bidialectal program has three major goals: (1) to create in students an awareness and acceptance of the value of more than one way of communicating; (2) to create in students an awareness that American society values individuals who can use Standard English communication skills in appropriate settings and an awareness of the impact upon educational, social, and economic goals of using the vernacular for all situations; and (3) to provide opportunities for students to practice mainstream communication skills to increase their communication repertoires. Federal Title I funds have been used for this program in seven schools with eligible fifth-, sixth-, seventh-, and eighth-grade students who are culturally and linguistically diverse, including speakers of vernacular dialects and students who have exited English as a second language (ESL) programs.

Professional development for teachers in the bidialectal program has involved an expanding teams approach. A speech-language pathologist with training in teaching reading and ESL developed, experimented with, and refined the program, then trained several expert classroom teachers over the period of a year. In the summer of 1998, a new model was tried out. The bidialectal program was delivered in a morning summer school program; in the afternoons, professional development was provided for teachers new to the program. These teachers teamed with program veterans in the morning classrooms.

Explicit teaching

Delpit (1995) argues that African American vernacular-speaking students demonstrate more success in meeting school-based expectations for interaction when teachers express directions, information, and intentions explicitly, using strong paralinguistic cues. In the bidialectal program, teachers give clear directives and concrete examples. They direct students to ask questions, explain, and offer rationales. They use cooperative learning environments, where language and communication thrive and where students seek outcomes that benefit others as well as themselves (Holubec, Johnson, & Johnson, 1994). Cooperative learning groups are established early in the school year, and students are directly taught the skills for commenting, commending, and critiquing in school-appropriate ways.

The bidialectal curriculum includes explicit knowledge about language and awareness of group-based differences. Teachers define and demonstrate metalinguistic thinking. They relate the techniques of literary analysis (i.e., identifying setting, plot, characters, and purposes) to speaking in order to help students develop a literate discourse style. For example, students who use African American vernacular exclusively often present oral stories in a topic associating style (Michaels, 1981). They may not explicitly state critical background information that is needed to make the meaning clear to a listener from another speech community. Teachers tell students directly that they cannot always assume that their listeners and readers know them and understand what they are talking about and that they have the responsibility for making their intentions clear to an unfamiliar audience.

This concept is introduced by using a highly familiar topic such as shopping for groceries. Teachers lead students in constructing a mind map (Margulies, 1991) where the central theme is represented pictorially. The teacher asks students for words that relate to the topic. As students name words, the teacher lists them in view of the class. Then the teacher asks students to identify the words associated with what must be done before going to the store (e.g., grocery list, money, food stamps, check book, transportation). These words are written in a bubble extension of the pictured theme. Next, the teacher asks for the words that are relevant during shopping (e.g., cart, aisles, coupons, cashier) and lists them in another bubble extension. Last, students identify the words that relate to tasks at the end of shopping. Using the mind map, teachers facilitate topic-centered narratives in which the theme is explicitly stated, subtopics are temporally ordered, topic shifts are encoded through transition words, supporting details are provided for each subtopic, nonessential information is eliminated, and a restatement of the theme occurs at the end (Michaels, 1981). Gradually the teacher fades use of such strategies and uses literature from the district's reading series for practicing topic-centered narratives.

The curriculum for the bidialectal program incorporates a contrastive analysis approach to developing students' explicit awareness of mainstream phonology and syntax. Students examine pairs of words and phrases that contrast minimally (e.g., *She done been here* vs. *She has been here*) and go on to develop minimal pairs from their reading. Students examine examples of syntactic forms that may contrast between dialects and that occur on standardized tests.

Teachers enhance students' awareness of other aspects of communication by using videotapes. One activity involves watching a video without the sound and guessing at what is going on based on nonverbal behavior alone. Students also learn to observe voice quality, intonation, and rate of speech.

Evaluation

Students in the DeKalb Bidialectal Communication Program participate in performance-based assessments throughout the school year conducted by their teachers and their cooperative group members. Students learn to listen to themselves and each other, to self-monitor, and to provide and use feedback (Latham, 1997) to shape their communication. Most assessment activities contrast home speech and school speech, and many involve role-plays. Students comment on the appropriateness of the language for the particular setting. Students are also videotaped at the beginning and end of the year reading a paragraph and telling a story. Teachers use the tapes to note the students' relative use of vernacular and standard dialect features. Teachers and students watch the tapes together and establish individual goals for language development. Taping at the end of the year allows them to see how close they came to meeting their goals. Teachers report that over time and without prompting from their teachers or peers, students begin to switch appropriately from home speech to school speech or the converse.

Test scores of students who have participated in the bidialectal program are impressive. Reading comprehension normal curve equivalent (NCE) scores on the Iowa Tests of Basic Skills show higher gains for students in this program than for comparable Title I students who are not in the program. Analyses of longitudinal data are being carried out.

Most of the students who have been in the program have reported that it gave them new information about language and helped them realize that their communication style was "good." Most of the parents whose children have been served through the program have expressed gratitude for it, and many have attended classes for parents on bidialectal communication.

Conclusion

The prospects for African American students' school success improve as teachers' abilities to provide appropriate instruction are enhanced. Basic to the success of a bidialectal model for African American students' language development has been the teachers' desire to learn more about their students and their families and communities. In the process of listening to students and learning about their homes and communities, teachers also learn about their language. Learning about students' language patterns by listening to them and through staff development enables teachers to work from a base of new understanding. Teachers in the bidialectal program are encouragers, listeners, and facilitators—not critics—of students' communication. These teachers are able to offer students appropriate, supportive feedback that facilitates language awareness and bidialectal development. What seems most appropriate about working toward bidialectalism is that it does not require students and families to make a choice between the language of the home and the language of school. In learning about conditions of time, place, manner, and situational appropriateness for oral communication, students and parents learn that there is room for all dialects in the schools.

Note

1. The author acknowledges Carolyn Adger for her supportive suggestions and comments on the draft of this manuscript. The author also acknowledges the expert teachers in the Title I-funded Bidialectal Communication Program in DeKalb County School System, Georgia: Isabelle Anderson, Lisa Brown, Joan Brown, Jeff Carter, Thomas Powell, and Christine Wood.

References

Adler, S. (1987, January). Bidialectalism: Mandatory or elective? *American Speech Language and Hearing Association*, 41-44.

Adler, S. (1993). *Multicultural communication skills in the classroom*. Boston: Allyn and Bacon.

Cazden, C. (1988). *Classroom discourse: The language of teaching and learning*. Portsmouth, NH: Heinemann.

Crago, M. B., Eriks-Brophy, A., McAlpine, L., & Pesco, D. (1997). Culturally based miscommunication in classroom interaction. *Language, Speech and Hearing Services in the Schools, 28*, 245-254.

Delpit, L. (1995). *Other people's children: Cultural conflict in the classroom*. New York: The New Press.

Harris-Wright, K. (1987). The challenge of educational coalescence: Teaching nonmainstream English-speaking students. *Journal of Childhood Communication Disorders, 11*(1), 209-215.

Holubec, E. J., Johnson, D. W., & Johnson, R. T. (1994). *The new circles of learning: Cooperation in the classroom and school*. Alexandria, VA: Association for Supervision and Curriculum Development.

Latham, A. S. (1997). Learning through feedback. *Educational Leadership, 54*(8), 86-87.

Margulies, N. (1991). *Mapping inner space: Learning and teaching mind mapping*. Tucson: Zephyr.

Michaels, S. (1981). "Sharing time": Children's narrative styles and differential access to literacy. *Language in Society, 10*, 423-442.

Perry, T., & Delpit, L. (Eds.). (1997). The real Ebonics debate: Power, language and the education of African American children [Special issue]. *Rethinking Schools, 12*(1).

Saravia-Shore, M., & Garcia, E. (1995). Diverse teaching strategies for diverse learners. In R. W. Cole (Ed.), *Educating everybody's children: Diverse teaching strategies for diverse learners* (pp. 47-74). Alexandria, VA: Association for Supervision and Curriculum Development.

Chapter 4

Repercussions From the Oakland Ebonics Controversy—The Critical Role of Dialect Awareness Programs

Walt Wolfram

If nothing else, the controversy and media blitz surrounding the Oakland (CA) resolution on Ebonics allows some important observations about the role of dialect differences in American society. First, the discussion has exposed the intensity of people's beliefs about language and language diversity. Beliefs and attitudes about language derive from the same core of beliefs that govern religion, morality, and ethics—all largely unassailable. In an important way, the Oakland resolution challenged underlying beliefs about the way language is supposed to be, thus leading to heated discussions of language that place it on a par with other controversial topics such as politics.

Second, the controversy bared the persistent and widespread level of public misinformation about language variation in education and public life. There is an entrenched mythology and miseducation about dialects, particularly with respect to the relationship between vernacular and standard varieties (Wolfram, Adger, & Christian, 1999; Wolfram & Schilling-Estes, 1998). Furthermore, the factual misinformation affects how we view people and how they view themselves on both a formal, institutional level and an informal, personal level. Operating on erroneous assumptions about language differences, it is easy for people to perpetuate unjustified stereotypes about language as it relates to class, ethnicity, and region. The consequences of misinformation about dialect diversity can thus be devastating for those who do not speak mainstream varieties.

Finally, the recent Ebonics controversy emphasized the need for greater knowledge about the facts of language diversity and its role in education and public life. Ironically, language diversity is one of the most fundamental dimensions of human behavior, yet there are few programs that educate students and the American population about it. The need for education about language diversity was highlighted in the resolution passed by the American Association for Applied Linguistics (1997), which noted that "all students and teachers should learn scientifically-based information about linguistic diversity," that "education should systematically incorporate information about language variation," and that linguists and other language professionals "should seek ways and means to better communicate the theories and principles of the field to the general public on a continuing basis."

In the following sections, I develop a rationale for increasing knowledge about language diversity through dialect awareness programs and suggest some themes for such programs. The term *dialect awareness* is used here to refer to activities that promote an understanding of and appreciation for language variation. It is my firm belief that extensive education about dialect diversity is the only way that we can guard against recycling public spectacles such as the one that surrounded the resolution of the Oakland School Board.

Although there are now sociolinguistic courses dealing with language diversity for students at the post-secondary level, the offerings still tend to be selective and optional, even for those who specialize in language-related disciplines such as language arts, speech and language pathology, and English as a second language. This is hardly enough. Education about language and language variation should not be limited to those who choose a university-based, optional course on this topic. There is an obvious need for knowledge about dialects for people at all levels of formal and informal education. Language variation affects us all, regardless of region, class, or ethnicity, and dialect awareness programs seem to be the only way to counter the destructive social, educational, and political effects of misguided notions about this phenomenon.

A Rationale for Dialect Awareness Programs

In this section, I set forth a rationale for dialect awareness programs and in the following one I offer some themes that should be part of such a program. It should be understood that these programs are different from, though not in opposition to, programs for teaching Standard English. In fact, I would argue that the most effective method for teaching Standard English would incorporate dialect awareness.

In light of the Ebonics controversy, it is also important to point out that such programs are not restricted to the consideration of African American Vernacular English. There exists a wide range of vernacular varieties of English as well as a range of regional standard dialects of English that need to be included in dialect awareness programs (Wolfram & Schilling-Estes, 1998). African American Vernacular English is a significant vernacular dialect with some special considerations because of the history of race relations in American society, but it is only one among many vernacular dialects. Misinformation and miseducation are hardly restricted to African American Vernacular English; there is considerable stereotyping about Appalachian dialects, Southern American English, and many ethnic varieties (e.g., Native American, Hispanic) in the United States. Dialect awareness programs should therefore represent the full array of language diversity in American society. In fact, experience with programs in schools and communities indicates that they are most effective and less threatening when they do not isolate a single language variety for discussion. I would thus suggest that an appropriate program includes the indigenous dialect of the community along with other representative varieties.

The rationale for dialect awareness programs is based in a commitment to search for fundamental truth about laws of nature and matter. With respect to language differences, there is an educational and societal tolerance of misinformation and folklore that is matched in few subject areas. An example is the widespread belief that only certain groups speak dialects and that these dialects are simply inadequate and inaccurate renditions of the standard variety. Such a belief clearly affects how the general public and teachers and other practitioners view and assess the language of vernacular-speaking students. Myths about the basis of language variation, the linguistic status of dialect structures, and the socioeducational implications of dialect divergence are deeply rooted in our educational system and society at large, and they need to be confronted as honestly as any other unjustified set of beliefs (Bauer & Trudgill, 1998). At the very least, then, dialect awareness programs are justified by the need to provide factual information about language variation to counter the entrenched mythology about language differences.

There are also issues of social and educational equity tied in with the need for accurate information about language differences. Operating on erroneous assumptions about language differences, people can easily fall prey to erroneous assessments about others' language capability as it reflects social factors such as class, race, and region. The potential for dialect discrimination cannot be taken more lightly than any other type of discrimination. Milroy and Milroy (1985) note:

> Although public discrimination on the grounds of race, religion and social class is not now publicly acceptable, it appears that discrimination on linguistic grounds is publicly acceptable, even though linguistic differences may themselves be associated with ethnic, religious and class differences. (p. 3)

This discrimination may operate in education, in the workplace, and in society at large. For example, a recent examination of the basis for assigning students to special education classes in a large metropolitan area showed that language traits were often cited as primary objective evidence of a need for special education, without any regard for the necessity to distinguish between language difference and language deficit (Adger, Wolfram, & Detwyler, 1994; Adger, Wolfram, Detwyler, & Harry, 1993). A socioeducational system that takes on the responsibility to educate students about racial and social differences and the effects of discrimination should feel obliged to extend this discussion to language as well.

The equity issue also supports a sociohistorical rationale for dialect awareness programs. As history and social studies texts strive to represent more fairly the contributions of various sociocultural groups to the development of the United States, it seems only reasonable to extend this requirement to language representation as well. A variety of vernacular dialects have influenced the development of American English, but there is little acknowledgement of this role. Nor is there any discussion of how different varieties have arisen and developed over time. For example, it is curious that the celebration of Black History Month rarely if ever includes any discussion of the historical development of African American Vernacular English, yet this is one of the most significant dialects of American English, historically and presently. Studying dialects provides a wealth of information on the historical and cultural contribution of various groups to American society, as well as on the dynamic nature of language.

Another rationale for these programs relates to the nature of intellectual inquiry. The study of dialects affords us a fascinating window through which to see how language works. The inner workings of language are just as readily observed in examining dialects and their patterning as they are through the exclusive study of a unitary standard variety. Language, including dialects, is a unique form of knowledge in that speakers know a language by virtue of the fact that they speak it. Much of this knowledge is not conscious, but it is still open to systematic investigation. Looking at dialect differences thus provides a natural laboratory for making generalizations from carefully described sets of data. We can hypothesize about the patterning of language features and then check our hypotheses on the basis of actual usage. This, of course, is a type of scientific inquiry.

This scientific rationale for studying dialects may seem a bit esoteric, but hypothesizing about and then testing language patterns is quite within the grasp of a wide age range of learners. I have led classes of students ages 9 through 11 through the steps of hypothesis formation and testing using exercises involving dialect features. I have also led informal groups of adult learners—such as participants at civic meetings, church meetings, and continuing education groups of all ages—through the same steps of inquiry. For example, the exercise on *a*-prefixing in the next section comes from an eighth-grade curriculum on dialects that I have taught in North Carolina, and it is also part of a curriculum we developed for an Elderhostel on dialects (Wolfram & Schilling-Estes, 1996). In a wide range of audiences, it has demonstrated inductively the detailed patterning of all dialects more effectively than sociolinguistic pontification.

Finally, there is a utilitarian reason for studying dialects. Information about dialects is helpful to individuals of all ages in developing the language skills required for success in education and formal social interaction, including the use of the standard variety. Vernacular dialect speakers may, for example, apply knowledge about dialect features to composing and editing their writing. I have witnessed students who studied structural features of language, such as -*s* third person absence in vernacular dialects (e.g., *She go to the store*), transfer this knowledge to writing Standard English. The study of various dialects hardly endangers the sovereignty of Standard English in the classroom. If anything, it enhances the learning of the standard variety through heightened sensitivity to language variation. It also places learning a standard variety in a more realistic context by making explicit the fundamental social and economic advantages of doing so.

Themes in a Dialect Awareness Program

Although it is beyond the scope of this chapter to offer an extensive set of activities and exercises that might be incorporated into a dialect awareness program (Wolfram & Creech, 1996; Wolfram, Dannenberg, Anderson, & Messner, 1996; Wolfram, Schilling-Estes, & Hazen, 1996), I suggest some major themes that should be included, especially since such programs are still relatively novel. Our own experimentation with dialect awareness programs in formal education has focused on the middle-school curriculum, but similar units can be developed for an upper-level elementary language arts curriculum and the secondary level as well. In informal education, I have designed programs that range from one-time, special-topic seminars and workshops to ongoing, community-based partnerships in continuing education for many different groups. The examples presented here are taken from my current work on the dialects of North Carolina.

Dialects are natural.

One theme that needs to be included in virtually all dialect awareness programs is the fundamental naturalness of dialect variation in American society. Participants need to confront stereotypes and misconceptions about dialects, but this is probably best done inductively, by having them listen to representative speech samples of regional, class, and ethnic varieties. They need to hear how native Standard English speakers in New England, the rural South, and urban North compare with each other and with the dialect of their own community to appreciate the reality of diverse regional spoken standards, just as they need to recognize different vernacular varieties in these regions. By examining the features of their own dialect as it compares with others, they may come to understand that everyone really does speak a dialect.

Although tape-recorded collections of dialect samples are not readily available, video productions like *American Tongues* (Alvarez & Kolker, 1987) can provide an entertaining introduction to dialects while at the same time exposing basic prejudices and myths about language differences. In one activity (Wolfram, Schilling-Estes, & Hazen,1996, p. 3), we have participants view real-life vignettes from *American Tongues* that expose raw prejudices about dialects. As participants reflect on the justness of the attitudes toward different dialects displayed in the video vignettes (taken from nonscripted, spontaneous footage), they confront stereotypes and prejudices about dialects and their speakers. It is not surprising that an evaluative summary of one of our dialect awareness programs (Messner, 1997) indicated that the learning experience participants cited most often concerned knowledge about prejudice and human relations related to dialect.

Participants can also examine cases of dialect variation from their own community to see how natural and inevitable dialects are. For example, virtually all communities have some local and regional lexical items that can be used as a starting point. We have developed activities on local lexical items such as the following, taken from *Dialects and the Ocracoke Brogue* (Wolfram, Schilling-Estes, & Hazen 1996).

OCRACOKE DIALECT VOCABULARY GAME: HOW TO TELL AN O'COCKER FROM A DINGBATTER

Fill in the blanks in the sentences below, choosing your answer from the list provided. You only have five minutes to complete the worksheet, and you may not look at the lexicon or share answers. At the end of five minutes, you will swap your book with a neighbor to check each other's work. For each correct answer, you will receive 1 point, and for each question missed, you will receive no points. Good luck.

WORD LIST: across the beach, buck, call the mail over, doast, good-some, meehonkey, miserable 'n the wind, mommuck, O'cocker, pizer, quamish, scud, slick cam, to, up the beach, yaupon

1. They went _____ to Hatteras to do some shopping.
2. Elizabeth is _____ the restaurant right now.
3. We took a _____ around the island in the car.
4. They're always together because he's his _____.
5. At night we used to play _____.
6. The ocean was so rough today I felt _____ in the gut.
7. Last night she came down with a _____.

8. They sat on the _____ in the evening.
9. You can't be an _____ unless you were born on the island.
10. The sea was real rough today; it was _____ out there.
11. When they _____ I hope I get my letter.
12. She used to _____ him when he was a child.
13. There was no wind at all today and it was a _____ out there on the sound.
14. There was a big, dead shark that they found _____.

Put a **1** by all the correct answers and an **X** by all the incorrect answers. Add up all of the correct answers and place the total in the blank. Hand the workbook back to its owner.

[Answers: 1. up the beach 2. to 3. scud 4. buck 5. meehonkey 6. quamished 7. doast 8. pizer 9. O'cocker ·10. miserable' n the wind 11. call the mail over 12. mommuck 13. slick cam 14. across the beach]

Such a simple vocabulary exercise underscores the dialect resources that reside in all varieties of a language regardless of social status. Learners themselves can take an active role in constructing dialect vocabulary exercises by helping to collect local lexical items. In the process, they learn to document dialect structures and determine the ways in which their local dialect is similar to and different from other varieties. In our studies of lexical items, community members have often taken leading roles in compiling community-based lexical inventories (e.g., Locklear, Schilling-Estes, Wolfram, & Dannenberg, 1996). Such collections emphasize the naturalness of dialect diversity and seize upon the natural curiosity that all people seem to have concerning different word uses.

Dialects are regular.

Another essential theme in dialect awareness concerns the patterning of dialect. It is essential for dialect awareness programs to combat the stereotype that vernacular varieties are nothing more than imperfect attempts to speak the standard variety. Since people tend to think of rules as prescriptive dicta that come from grammar books rather than from natural language usage, an inductive exercise on the systematic nature of dialects can help to generate a nonpatronizing respect for the complexity of systematic differences among dialects. I have used the following exercise on the patterning of *a*-prefixing (Wolfram, 1980) hundreds of times in all types of formal and informal discussions to demonstrate the fundamental patterning of all dialects regardless of social position. Since it involves a form whose pattern is intuitively accessible to English speakers, whether they use the form in their own dialect or not (Wolfram, 1982), it is appropriate for everyone. Sections of this exercise are reprinted from one of our curricula designed for middle school students (Wolfram, Schilling-Estes, & Hazen, 1996).

AN EXERCISE IN DIALECT PATTERNING

In historically isolated rural dialects of the United States, particularly in Southern Appalachia, some words that end in -*ing* can take an *a*-, pronounced as *uh*, attached to the beginning of the word. We call this the *a*- prefix because it attaches to the front of the -*ing* word. The language pattern or "rule" for this form allows the *a*- to attach to some words but not to others. In this exercise, you will figure out this fairly complicated rule by looking at the kinds of -*ing* words *a*- can and cannot attach to. You will do this using your inner feelings about language. These inner feelings, called *intuitions*, tell us where we can and cannot use certain features. As linguists trying to describe this dialect, our task is to figure out the reason for these inner feelings and to state the exact patterns that characterize the dialect.

Look at the sentence pairs in List A and decide which sentence in each pair sounds better with an *a*- prefix. For example, in the first sentence pair, does it sound better to say, "A-building is hard work" or "He was a-building a house"? For each sentence pair, just choose one sentence that sounds better with the *a*-.

LIST A: Sentence Pairs for *A*- Prefixing

1. a. __ Building is hard work.
   b. __ She was building a house.
2. a. __ He likes hunting.
   b. __ He went hunting.

3. a. __ The child was charming the adults.
   b. __ The child was very charming.
4. a. __ He kept shocking the children.
   b. __ The story was shocking.
5. a. __ They thought fishing was easy.
   b. __ They were fishing this morning.
6. a. __ The fishing is still good here.
   b. __ They go fishing less now.

Examine each of the sentence pairs in terms of the choices for the a- prefix and answer the following questions.

• Do you think there is some pattern that guided your choice of an answer? You can tell if there is a definite pattern by checking with other people who did the same exercise on their own.

• Do you think that the pattern might be related to parts of speech? To answer this, see if there are any parts of speech where you *cannot* use the a- prefix. Look at -ing forms that function as verbs and compare those with -ing forms that operate as nouns or adjectives. For example, look at the use of *charming* as a verb and adjective in sentence 3.

[List B, omitted here, is used to determine whether the a- form can occur in prepositional phrases.]

Another part to the pattern for a- prefix use is related to pronunciation. For the following -ing words, try to figure out what it is about the pronunciation that makes one sentence sound better than the other. To help you figure out the pronunciation trait that is critical for this pattern, the stressed or accented syllable of each word is marked with the symbol ´. Follow the same procedure that you did in choosing the sentence in each sentence pair that sounds better.

LIST C: Figuring out a Pronunciation Pattern for the A- Prefix

1. a. __ She was discóvering a trail.
   b. __ She was fóllowing a trail.
2. a. __ She was repéating the chant.
   b. __ She was hóllering the chant.

Say exactly how the pattern for attaching the *a-* prefix works. Be sure to include the three different details from your examination of the examples in **LISTS A, B, and C.**

In **LIST D**, say which of the sentences may take an *a-* prefix. Use your understanding of the rule to explain why the *-ing* form may or may not take the *a-* prefix.

LIST D: Applying the *A-* Prefix Rule

1. She kept handing me more work.
2. The team was remémbering the game.
3. The team was playing real hard.
4. The coach was charming.

(from Wolfram, Schilling-Estes, & Hazen, 1996, pp. 23-26)

Exercises of this type effectively confront the myth that dialects have no rules of their own. At the same time, they demonstrate the underlying cognitive patterning of language. The most effective approach to dialect patterning includes examples from local, community-based dialects as well as examples from other regional and ethnic dialects. We have used the *a*-prefixing exercise with the following exercise on the habitual *be* construction of African American Vernacular English in dialect awareness programs for both Northern inner-city groups that are predominantly African American and Southern rural groups that are predominantly Anglo American.

BE IN AFRICAN AMERICAN ENGLISH

Now we're going to look at a form in a dialect that is sometimes used by young African American speakers in large cities. The form *be* is used where other dialects use *am, is,* or *are,* except that it has a special meaning. People who use this dialect can tell where it may be used and where it may not be used, just like you did for the *a-* prefix. In the sentences given here, choose one of the sentences in each pair where *be* fits better. Choose only one sentence for each pair. If you're not sure of the answer, simply make your best guess. Put a check next to the answer you think is right. *Do this work by yourself.*

1. a. __ They usually be tired when they come home.
   b. __ They be tired right now.
2. a. __ When we play basketball, she be on my team.
   b. __ The girl in the picture be my sister.
3. a. __ James be coming to school right now.
   b. __ James always be coming to school.
4. a. __ Wanda don't usually be in school.
   b. __ Wanda don't be in school today.
5. a. __ My ankle be broken from the fall.
   b. __ Sometimes my ears be itching.

Now that you've given your answers, you'll see a video of some speakers of this dialect doing the same exercise. How well did you do on the exercise compared to these students in the video who regularly use the *be* form?

Following the Patterns for *Be* Use

Now that you know how the form *be* is used, predict which of the sentences below follow the rule for *be* use in the African American English dialect and which do not. Write **(Y)**es if the sentence follows the dialect pattern and **(N)**o if it doesn't.

1. __ The students always be talking in class.
2. __ The students don't be talking right now.
3. __ Sometimes the teacher be early for class.
4. __ At the moment the teacher be in the lounge.
5. __ Linguists always be asking silly questions about language.

(from Wolfram, Schilling-Estes, & Hazen, 1996, p. 26)

We also use examples of dialect patterning from regional varieties to complement the focus on the vernacular-standard distinction highlighted in the preceding exercises. This helps students understand the interaction of region, class, and ethnicity in the distribution of dialect patterns. Following is an exercise on the patterning of postvocalic *r* in Eastern New England, where it is a frequent though not exclusive regional phenomenon.

HOW PRONUNCIATION DIFFERENCES WORK: DROPPING *R* IN NEW ENGLAND SPEECH

In New England and some other dialects of English, including some dialects of African American Vernacular English, the *r* sound of words like *car* or *poor* can be dropped. In these words, the *r* is not pronounced, so that these words sound like *cah* and *poh*. However, not all *r* sounds can be dropped. In some places in a word, the *r* sound may be dropped and in other places it may not be dropped. By comparing lists of words where the *r* may be dropped with lists of words where it may not be dropped, we can figure out a pattern for *r*-dropping.

List B gives words where the *r* sound may **NOT** be dropped. In other words, speakers who drop their *r*'s in List A pronounce the *r* in the words in List B.

LIST A	LIST B
1. car	1. *r*un
2. father	2. bring
3. card	3. principal
	4. app*r*oach

To find a pattern for dropping the *r*, look at the type of sound that comes before the *r* in List A and in List B. Does a vowel or a consonant come before the *r* in List A? What comes before the *r* in List B? How can you predict where an *r* may or may not be dropped?

In List C, pick those words that may drop their *r* and those that may not drop their *r*. Use your knowledge of the *r*-dropping pattern that you learned by comparing List A and B.

LIST C
_____ 1. bear
_____ 2. program
_____ 3. fearful
_____ 4. right

Think of two new words that may drop an *r* and two new words that may not drop an *r*.

MORE ABOUT *R*-DROPPING PATTERNS

In the last exercise we saw that *r* dropping only takes place when the *r* comes after a vowel.

Now we are going to look at the kinds of sounds that may come after the *r* in some dialects of English. This pattern goes along with the one you already learned. Let's see if we can figure out the pattern.

Here are some words where the *r* may not be dropped even when it comes after a vowel.

List A: Words that do NOT drop *R*
>   1. bear in the field
>   2. car over at the house
>   3. garage

What kinds of sounds come after the *r* in List A? Are they vowels or consonants?

In List B the *r* MAY be dropped. What kind of sounds come after the *r* in this list?

List B: Words that drop *R*
>   1. bear by the woods
>   2. car parked by the house
>   3. parking the bus

How does this pattern or rule for *r*-dropping work in terms of sounds that come after *r*?

Use your knowledge of the rule for *r*-dropping to pick the *r*'s that may and may not be dropped in the sentence given below.
>   1. The teacher picked on three students for an answer.
>   2. Four cars parked far away from the fair.

(from Wolfram, Schilling-Estes, & Hazen, 1996, pp. 16-18)

The advantages of these types of exercises should be obvious. Learners see how linguists collect and organize data to formulate the rules that describe language patterning. More importantly, students come to appreciate the intricate details of patterning in language variation. Such exercises may also provide a model for analyzing data that students collect from their own community. When learners record language data, extract particular examples, and formulate linguistic rules themselves, they experience firsthand the examination of language in a rigorous, scientific way.

In addition to viewing dialect study as scientific investigation, learners should be encouraged to see how dialect study merges with the social sciences and the humanities. Dialect study can be viewed from the perspective of geography, history, or sociology; it also can be linked with ethnic or gender studies.

In examining the role of dialect as a dimension of social history, it is important to provide a general perspective on language change as well as a local, community, or regional vantage point. The model program discussed here focuses on a number of details of dialect patterning for Okracoke while also including features of other dialects to show that all dialects, not just Ocracoke, are systematic. Our pilot program for Baltimore, Maryland, which targeted a student population of African American Vernacular English speakers (Wolfram, Detwyler, & Adger, 1992), focused on the structures common to this student population while also including samples from other dialects, such as New England or Appalachian English. It is important for students to study their own dialect features, but it is also essential to extend the study to other, nonlocal varieties of English so that students understand that the principles that they are studying apply to all varieties, not just the ones they speak.

We also use activities that demonstrate how the English language in general is evolving over time.

THE CHANGING OF THE ENGLISH LANGUAGE

English has changed quite dramatically over the centuries. In fact, if we go back far enough, we can barely recognize the language as English. Compare the versions of English at various stages in its history, as found in the first verse of the Lord's Prayer.

Old English (about 950 A.D.)

Fader urer ðu bist in heofnas, sie gehalgad noma ðin

Middle English (about 1350 A.D.)

Oure fadir þat art in heuenes, halwid be þi name

Early Modern English (about 1550 A.D.)

O oure father which arte in heven, hallowed be thy name

Modern English (about 1985 A.D.)

Our father, who is in heaven, may your name be sacred

>   or

Our father, who art in heaven, hallowed be your name

1. Try pronouncing the different versions of English. In the older versions (Old and Middle English), silent letters do not exist, so you'll need to pronounce all the letters. The symbol ð is pronounced something like the *th* of *this*, and the þ is pronounced like the *th* of *think*.

2. Try to identify some of the older versions of modern words. For example, trace the words that became the current words *father*, *heaven*, *name*, *is*, and *our*. What modern English word, besides *sacred*, did *hallow* become?

3. What does this comparison tell you about the way the English language has changed over the centuries?

One of the greatest advantages of the examination of dialects is its potential for tapping the language resources of learners' communities. Participants can learn by going into the community to collect live data that make dialects come alive. A model that builds upon community resources in language, even when the language is different from the norm of the educational system, seems to hold much greater potential for success than one that focuses exclusively upon language conflicts between the community and school.

Community-Based Collaboration— The Ocracoke Model

The Oakland controversy points out the need for educating the general American public in a variety of formal and informal venues.

Our own efforts to promote dialect awareness have included the formal classroom but have also moved beyond it to establish community-based programs that involve informal education. These include TV and video documentaries (e.g., Alvarez & Kolker, 1987; Blanton & Waters, 1995; Creech & Creech, 1996); trade books on dialects for general audiences (Wolfram & Schilling-Estes, 1997); museum exhibits (Gruendler, Holden, Wolfram, & Schilling-Estes, 1997); and presentations to community organizations such as civic groups, churches, preservation societies, and other local institutions and agencies. Involvement with local communities on the Outer Banks of North Carolina, whose dialects are in a moribund, or dying, state (Wolfram & Schilling-Estes, 1995), includes work with the Ocracoke Preservation Society.

The venues we use to disseminate information include both traditional and nontraditional agencies. In addition to the dialect program in the Ocracoke School, we have made presentations to the Ocracoke Historical Preservation Society and to various visitors' groups on Ocracoke. We have even shown our documentary several times at the local bar and grill, Howard's Pub, where residents and tourists typically congregate. These showings resulted in animated, positive discussions about the dialect by both Ocracoke residents and tourists. The endangered status of the Ocracoke brogue has also been the subject of several local, regional, and even international television and radio news programs, and there were at least a dozen major feature articles in local and regional newspapers from 1992 to 1998 that focused on the state of the dialect and the threats to its survival. Several of these stories were accompanied by sound bites; readers were invited to call an advertised telephone number and listen to a recorded sample of the brogue. The *Virginian Pilot* newspaper reported that more readers called in to hear the sample of the brogue than any other sound bite they had made available.

Although I have presented our community-based dialect awareness programs as a model, I must admit that community-based collaboration raises deeper issues about the roles of sociolinguistic researchers in local communities (Rickford, 1997). In principle, few sociolinguists would probably be opposed to working with local communities in dialect awareness programs, but working out the details of this relationship and the exact nature of community-based partnerships can be complicated and controversial. There are ideological, sociopolitical, and ethical matters that need to be confronted squarely by linguists and sociolinguists who engage in such programs (Wolfram, 1993, in press). These include issues of authority, power, representation, presentation, and profit. Nonetheless, the concept of working with communities and returning linguistic favors to those who have provided linguistic data in some form seems to be a good and proper thing. It also seems to be the least that linguists and sociolinguists can do when we consider how we have mined so many of the speech community's linguistic resources to our professional advantage.

Conclusion

The Oakland situation has clearly demonstrated the inherent interest and concern that most people have about language issues as well as the need for public education on these issues. As the superintendent of the Oakland Schools, Carolyn Getridge, noted, this situation created "a teachable moment of national proportion" (1997)—an occasion to provide accurate information about dialect diversity to counter some of the misguided popular interpretations portrayed in the early media accounts. It gave me personally, along with a number of my colleagues, an unprecedented opportunity to present information about the natural, legitimate base of language variation to a wide range of audiences. We have needed to seize the moment to provide sociolinguistic service to the American public. And from this point, we need to move forward to implement dialect awareness programs for schools and the general public that will eventually lead to the replacement of widespread, destructive myths about language variation with scientific evidence on the nature of dialect diversity. It is perhaps our only hope for a more equitable and more enlightened future in which contentious debate over natural, inevitable dialect diversity will have no place in our society.

References

Adger, C. T., Wolfram, W., & Detwyler, J. (1994). Enhancing delivery of services to Black special education students from non-standard English backgrounds (Final Report). Washington, DC: U.S. Department of Education, Office of Special Education Programs. Cooperative Agreement No. HO23400008-92.

Adger, C. T., Wolfram, W., Detwyler, D., & Harry, B. (1993). Confronting dialect minority issues in special education: Reactive and proactive perspectives. In *Third national research symposium on limited English students' issues* (pp. 737-762). Washington, DC: U.S. Government Printing Office.

Alvarez, L., & Kolker, A. (Producers). (1987). *American tongues.* New York: Center for New American Media.

American Association for Applied Linguistics. (1997). *Resolution on the application of dialect knowledge to education.* Annual Meeting of AAAL, Orlando, FL.

Bauer, L., & Trudgill, P. (Eds.). (1998). *Language myths.* New York: Penguin.

Blanton, P., & Waters, K. (Producers). (1995). *The Ocracoke Brogue.* Raleigh, NC: North Carolina Language and Life Project.

Creech, K., & Creech, J. (Producers). (1996). *That island talk: Harkers Island Dialect.* Raleigh, NC: American Media Productions and the North Carolina Language and Life Project.

Ebonics: Hearing before the Subcommittee on Labor, Health and Human Services, and Education, of the Senate Committee on Appropriations, 105th Cong., 1st Sess. (1997) (testimony of Carolyn M. Getridge).

Gruendler, S., Holden, C., Wolfram, W., & Schilling-Estes, N. (1997). An exhibit on the Ocracoke Brogue. Ocracoke, NC: The Museum of the Ocracoke Preservation Society.

Locklear, H. A., Schilling-Estes, N., Wolfram, W., & Dannenberg, C. (1996). *A dialect dictionary of Lumbee English.* Raleigh, NC: North Carolina Language and Life Project.

Messner, K. (1997). Evaluative summary of Appalachian Dialect Awareness program. Unpublished report. Boone, NC: Appalachian State University.

Milroy, J., & Milroy, L. (1985). *Authority in language: Investigating language prescriptivism and standardization.* London: Routledge & Kegan.

Rickford, J. R. (1997). Unequal partnerships: Sociolinguistics and the African American speech community. *Language in Society, 26,* 161-197.

Wolfram, W. (1980). A-prefixing in Appalachian English. In W. Labov (Ed.), *Locating language in time and space* (pp. 107-43). New York: Academic Press.

Wolfram, W. (1982). Language knowledge and other dialects. *American Speech, 57*, 3-17.

Wolfram, W. (1993). Ethical considerations in language awareness programs. *Issues in Applied Linguistics, 4*, 225-255.

Wolfram, W. (in press). Deconstructing linguistic gratuity. *Journal of Sociolinguistics.*

Wolfram, W., Adger, C. T., & Christian. D. (1999). *Dialects in schools and communities.* Mahweh, NJ: Erlbaum.

Wolfram, W., & Creech, K. (1996). *Harkers Island speech and dialects* (8th grade curriculum, Harkers Island School, Carteret County, NC). Raleigh, NC: North Carolina Language and Life Project.

Wolfram, W., Dannenberg, C., Anderson, B., & Messner, K. (1996). *Dialects and Appalachian English* (8th grade curriculum, Mabel School, Watauga County, NC). Raleigh, NC: North Carolina Language and Life Project.

Wolfram, W., Detwyler, J., & Adger, C.T. (1992). *All about dialects* (Instructor's Manual). Washington, DC: Center for Applied Linguistics.

Wolfram, W., & Schilling-Estes, N. (1995). Moribund dialects and the endangerment canon: The case of the Ocracoke Brogue. *Language, 71,* 696-721.

Wolfram, W., & Schilling-Estes, N. (1996). Speech at the beach: Dialects and Outer Banks English. An Elderhostel course of study at the Trinity Center, Salter Path, NC.

Wolfram, W., & Schilling-Estes, N. (1997). *Hoi toide on the Outer Banks: The story of the Ocracoke Brogue.* Chapel Hill, NC: University of North Carolina Press.

Wolfram, W. & Schilling-Estes, N. (1998). *American English: Dialects and variation.* Cambridge: Basil Blackwell.

Wolfram, W., Schilling-Estes, N., & Hazen, K. (1996). *Dialects and the Ocracoke Brogue* (8th grade curriculum, Ocracoke School, Hyde County, NC). Raleigh, NC: North Carolina Language and Life Project.

Chapter 5

Considerations in Preparing Teachers for Linguistic Diversity[1]

John Baugh

During Senate testimony on January 23, 1997, in the wake of the Oakland (CA) School Board's announcement of their Ebonics policy, Orlando Taylor, Dean of the Graduate School of Arts and Sciences at Howard University (and co-editor of this volume), observed that much of the vitriolic reaction toward Oakland educators had been misplaced. Taking a position that they later recanted, the Oakland Board had called for a linguistic reclassification of African American students as "Ebonics speakers." Taylor correctly remarked that not all African American students are Ebonics speakers, and African American students are not the only ones who speak nonstandard English (*Ebonics,* 1997). Whereas the Oakland Ebonics resolution focused on the linguistic status and educational plight of students who are American slave descendants, Taylor attempted to broaden the discussion to include other groups. In so doing, he echoed Geneva Smitherman and others affiliated with the Conference on College Composition and Communication (CCCC) of the National Council of Teachers of English (NCTE) who advocate a national language policy that encourages all students—regardless of race or social status—to learn a second language or second dialect beyond their native one (Conference on College Composition and Communication, 1988).

Following in the tradition of Taylor and the CCCC, I approach the topic of language diversity and African American student achievement in a broader context. My concern is with preparing teachers for dialect diversity. Educating teachers to recognize and overcome educational inequities tied to language differences is an important undertaking. While this discussion focuses on issues regarding African American students who do not speak or write Standard American English, we must bear in mind that many students who are not descendants of American slaves may also encounter linguistic barriers to academic achievement. Teacher education must deal with the full picture in order to move toward improving the linguistic knowledge, skills, and attitudes of teachers and teacher candidates. Here I explore some issues for teacher education that need to be resolved to make schools dialectally equitable.

The Issue of Terminology

In alluding to the Ebonics debate, definition of terms may be helpful. One reason is that the Oakland School Board's position involved a definition of *language* that led to controversy. Another is that participants in the public conversation that followed used terms to mean different things. Further, linguists' terminology that I use here is not widely shared outside linguistics. I use three terms somewhat interchangeably (largely for stylistic reasons): Standard English, mainstream American English, and the dialect of wider communication. For linguists, these terms are intended to be descriptive and free of any social value judgment, but many nonlinguists have interpreted Standard English as being synonymous with correct English or proper English, which are loaded, judgmental terms that professional linguists seek to avoid. It is partially for this reason that scholars have introduced alternative terms.

It is understandable that many nonlinguists have come to define Standard English in these value-laden terms. The attitudes toward language diversity that they encode have not been successfully challenged in schools, despite the fact that they have no basis in scientific fact. From a linguistic point of view, the standard varieties are not superior to nonstandard varieties of English. Linguists' declarations of dialect neutrality often strike members of the general public as absurd or perhaps naive, because the influential, prescribed varieties of English are sanctioned and reinforced in professional and academic contexts. But linguistic research has established that nonstandard dialects are as coherent, logical, complex, and systematic as the socially dominant standard dialects, despite uninformed linguistic opinion that demeans nonstandard English.

These definitional contrasts evoke the dilemma that teachers and teacher educators face. The overwhelming social stereotypes that presume nonstandard English to be inferior to mainstream American English, despite linguistic evidence to the contrary, have practical consequences for those who seek employment, housing, or academic advancement where gatekeepers lack linguistic tolerance—or worse.

There is no consensus on what to call the linguistic consequences of the African slave trade. Linguists have used the terms *vernacular Black English* or *Black English,* but during the 1980s those terms were generally replaced by *African American Vernacular English. Ebonics,* coined by Williams (1975) to refer to the linguistic consequences of the African slave trade in West Africa, the Caribbean, and the United States, was not generally used by linguists. In the context of the controversy arising from Oakland's language policy, linguists have generally equated Ebonics with African American Vernacular English (e.g., Rickford, 1997). However, some scholars prefer the term Ebonics and claim that it is the antithesis of Black English (Smith, 1992). Readers should recognize that *Ebonics* is defined in different ways.

Linguistic Understandings and Teacher Education

What, then, can we tell teachers about language that might enhance their capacity to teach the dialect of wider communication to Black students? What linguistic information do they need in order to better understand that African American speech patterns are not merely a corrupt form of Standard English, but the result of combined linguistic, educational, legal, and social policies that were intended to restrict the literacy of slaves and the educational opportunities of their descendants? (See Vaughn-Cooke, this volume). How do we point out essential linguistic differences between the nonstandard English of slave descendants and the nonstandard English of Native Americans and immigrants whose ancestors were never enslaved in America? There are no straightforward technical answers to these questions. If there were, teacher education would already be addressing the problems of linguistic inequality more comprehensively and effectively, and the society would be moving toward linguistic homogenization or greater acceptance of linguistic diversity—or perhaps both.

In pointing out that approaches to teaching teachers about linguistic diversity are not well known, I do not want to imply that teacher preparation programs are justified in giving short shrift to language diversity. While linguistic prejudice represents an unfortunate form of sociolinguistic pathology, it takes on a particularly destructive form among teachers, student teachers, and teacher educators who conclude that students who do not speak mainstream

American English have cognitive deficiencies or that they lack the capacity for abstract thought (Farrell, 1983). The job of preparing teachers for linguistic diversity must be viewed in the context of factors that have prohibited the wholesale eradication of linguistic bias in education. Four factors that especially affect African American students will be considered in the remainder of this discussion: fiscal constraints, restrictive policies, misguided liberalism, and lingering racial and linguistic stereotypes.

Fiscal Constraints

Educational funding for public schools is tied to local property taxes. Unlike many other advanced industrialized societies, the United States does not have a central Ministry of Education to coordinate education nationally, and it produces combinations of the best and worst public schools in the world. The best schools tend to be well funded, with high levels of parental involvement and consistent leadership; the worst schools tend to have fewer financial resources, overcrowded classrooms, too many inexperienced teachers, and little in the way of coherent leadership, often with minimum parental involvement or support.

Because slaves were historically denied access to schools and the courts as well as to the economic opportunities that enhance prospects for personal and family development, the education of African Americans has never been comparable to or competitive with that of residents who do not share the historical legacy of racialized educational disenfranchisement that continues to plague the academic welfare of far too many Black students. Comer (1997) points to two myths that are relevant to negative stereotypes about African Americans and our educational achievements—or lack thereof. The first such myth is that all U.S. citizens have equal opportunity: Those who work hard excel, and those who are lazy decline and fail. The second myth is that differences in achievement have their basis in genetics: Those who inherit "good genes" will simply outperform those with "inferior genes."

These stereotypes tend to be perpetuated by inequitable educational resource allocations that particularly affect slave descendants, many of whom have attended inferior schools. For those policy makers who accept the "genetic deficiency hypothesis" as espoused in *The Bell Curve* (Herrnstein & Murray, 1994), there is no reason to allocate funds on a more equitable basis than the amount of local property taxes in order to increase educational funding for populations that are perceived to be unwilling or unable to take full advantage of the additional resources.

Another fiscal consideration concerns the investment in teacher education. At most institutions of higher learning that offer state-approved teacher certification programs, resource allocations for teacher preparation are dwarfed by the financial support for the preparation of other professionals, such as accountants and engineers (at the undergraduate level) or attorneys and scientists (at the professional or graduate school level) (Melnick & Zeichner, 1997).

I confess a degree of professional frustration and envy as a former director of Stanford's teacher education program: frustration because we only had one year to prepare secondary school teachers and envy because my colleagues in business, law, and medicine were, by comparison, flush with ample funding, equipment, support, and time to prepare their graduates to enter their respective professions. At the same time, however, I experienced great joy in the countless wonderful experiences with student teachers who were selfless and dedicated to the future welfare of their students. Material gain was not driving their professional aspirations, and I found that trait very appealing.

Many higher education administrators feel that they cannot insist on longer programs of study for student teachers who, unlike physicians and attorneys, will enter a profession with comparatively low salaries. Despite the recognition that teacher education might benefit from extended or expanded programs, many college officials feel that the cost of such expansion would deter students from entering the teaching profession in the first place. Within these parameters, it becomes nearly impossible to add courses that would counteract misperceptions and prejudices regarding language diversity. Indeed, linguistic education for prospective teachers competes with other curricular innovations. Thus the past becomes increasingly immutable.

Restrictive Policies

The preceding discussion hints at some of the policy problems endemic to America's educational enterprise that bear especially on the school achievement of African American children. The national ethos that every child has a right to a free public education is undermined by the lack of political will to extend that right to ensure that every child has the finest possible education. It is largely for this reason that many private schools flourish despite the availability of free public education. They survive or fail based on their ability to attract paying customers with the promise of a superior product. I hasten to point out that some private schools are dismal; it would be misleading to imply that private schools are inherently superior to public schools, because "that just ain't so." However, private schools are unregulated by local, state, or federal educational mandates, whereas public schools must conform to layer upon layer of regulation.

At this writing, there is extensive public debate regarding the relative value of school vouchers, bilingual education, and affirmative action, all of which are controversial and all of which are embroiled in legislative contortions that have a direct or indirect impact on the quality of education in many public schools throughout the country. In my home state of California, for example, we face an ironic contradiction: Bilingual education and other programs intended to educate language minority students have been deregulated throughout the state; however, pending ballot measures call for specific restrictions on bilingual education, including pedagogical approach and length of participation. This legislation will be felt more strongly in the poorer schools and school districts that teach larger numbers of language minority students and will leave virtually untouched the affluent schools with few language minority students.

The Ebonics controversy sparked in Oakland, which provided the impetus for the chapters in this volume, also points to some of the overt and covert restrictions on the education of African American students.[2] The linguistic consequences of slavery and the legacy of educational apartheid that have afflicted generations of African Americans have never been adequately resolved. The linguistic dimension was the object of Oakland's highly visible Ebonics venture. Oakland educators were caught in a restrictive policy paradox some years in the making.

In the wake of the Ann Arbor Black English trial in 1979 (see *The Ann Arbor Decision,* n.d.; Whiteman, 1980), the California State Department of Education authorized a program to enhance the development of Standard English proficiency for speakers of "Black language." The Standard English Proficiency Program was inaugurated in 1981 to offer educators throughout California information on ways to increase Standard English proficiency among African American students.

By contrast, the federal government has never formally acknowledged that African American Vernacular English (AAVE) is a barrier to academic success. Although Ann Arbor Judge Charles Joiner ruled in favor of the African American plaintiffs in 1979, thereby confirming that AAVE does represent a language barrier to academic success, the defendant school district did not appeal his ruling. Thus the regional relevance and legal authority of the ruling was limited. Unlike *Brown v. Board of Education* (1954), the Ann Arbor Black English case did not advance to the Supreme Court.

The regulatory paradox that Oakland educators faced, then, placed them between California's Standard English Program, which did acknowledge that many African American students require special linguistic education, and federal policies that essentially blocked formal recognition of AAVE as a language minority concern. U.S. Secretary of Education Richard Riley strongly condemned the Ebonics resolution, stating adamantly that no Title VII (bilingual education) funding would be forthcoming for students who speak "Black English" (a possibility suggested early on to help these students become bilingual). He failed to offer positive suggestions or support, however, to those teachers who strive to help students gain greater Standard English proficiency.

This lack of federal leadership regarding linguistic diversity is not being compensated for in teacher preparation. Very few teacher education programs address these issues. Some of this failure comes from restrictive state mandates regarding the number and kind of required courses that must be completed by student teachers to obtain teaching certification. Often there is simply insufficient flexibility to allow students to learn the knowledge and skills that they need regarding their students' language. The fiscal underpinnings for this situation were indicated in the previous section.

Policy makers in state and federal educational agencies and administrators of teacher education programs must find ways to provide greater flexibility so that in-service teachers and pre-service teachers can learn more about the history of linguistic diversity in the United States and how to teach students from diverse language backgrounds effectively. These problems are especially pronounced in California, Florida, New York, Texas, and other states that have rapidly growing populations of nonnative speakers of English or other minority populations for whom Standard English is not native.

Misguided Liberalism

Although there is a pervasive belief that racial prejudice and antiminority sentiment have accentuated gaps between the educational performance of affluent students and that of less affluent students, misguided liberalism has also contributed to the academic abyss through well-intended programs that do little more than maintain the achievement status quo. I agree with Darling-Hammond's (1994) observations that Teach for America and some other well-meaning programs that claim to help the poor are woefully ineffective despite their laudable intentions.

Teach for America began at Princeton University when a graduating senior, Wendy Kopp, wrote a thesis calling for college graduates to devote 2 years of their lives to teaching for the poor. The notion was modeled after the Peace Corps. Given the limited resources and teacher shortages that confront many poor, rural, and inner-city schools, Kopp suggested that bright, energetic college graduates could help by offering to teach students in schools and districts with limited resources. Teach For America candidates participate in an intensive summer training program before they are placed in their own classrooms throughout the country.

Darling-Hammond and other professional educators were extremely frustrated by suggestions that poor students would be taught by inexperienced teachers. Those who are familiar with the circumstances confronting inner-city and rural schools with limited resources will appreciate that they represent some of the most difficult and challenging assignments that any teacher could ever face. These schools desperately need experienced professionals to provide academic enrichment. But because these are the very school districts that have limited funding, they are not able to offer high salaries that might attract more experienced teachers.

I am somewhat sympathetic to Kopp's good intentions and to those of the young graduates who share her willingness to briefly devote time to teaching poor students. However, as a linguist and educator who has devoted a lifetime to the quest for social equity, I share a greater concern for those students who have become experimental fodder for a program that would never be tolerated by parents of affluent students. We know that inexperienced teachers are more likely to be successful with students whose backgrounds are quite similar to their own (Bridges, 1992). Would advocates of Teach For America consider a slight programmatic modification: namely, allowing Teach For America candidates to teach in affluent communities? Under this modified scenario, Teach For America candidates would still go through their intensive summer training, but rather than teaching the poor, they would replace experienced teachers in affluent schools, thereby allowing experienced teachers (who were willing) to teach in inner-city or rural schools, and to do so without any loss in pay. Although I have no direct evidence to confirm my suspicion, I suspect that many affluent parents who would support Teach For America for poor students would have profound objections to having their own children taught by Teach For America candidates in order to provide more experienced teachers for the poor.

I wish to echo Darling-Hammond's (1994) observations, which are reinforced by Comer (1997), Hollins (1996), and Ladson-Billings (1994), all of whom call for innovative ways to enhance teacher professionalism as we strive to close the academic gaps that remind us that America has yet to fully achieve her color-blind ambition.

Lingering Racial and Linguistic Stereotypes

During the 2 years that I served as director of Stanford's teacher education program, I became aware that many of our student teachers harbored linguistic and racial stereotypes about low-income and minority students. The most pronounced evidence of this came in the form of comments about African American and Mexican American students as incapable and linguistically incoherent and about Asian American students as being gifted in math and science.

In what was for me a wonderful collaboration, anthropologist and ethnographer Ray McDermott and I devoted considerable attention to dispelling some of the false linguistic and racial assumptions that many Stanford student teachers brought with them to our teacher education program. We had the good fortune to establish a special summer school that served middle school and high school students from diverse backgrounds, drawing pupils from several school districts. We were able to create small classes where outstanding mentor teachers worked closely with four student teachers in various subjects, including math, science, English, foreign language, and social studies. Applying the content of our graduate course to their teaching, we challenged and refuted some stereotypes that, if unchecked, could have been detrimental to the student teachers and their pupils. Since then I have had several opportunities to meet with experienced teachers and student teachers in other parts of the country. The Ebonics controversy broke the silence of many educators who simply had not expressed their deep concerns or reservations about the language that African American students bring with them to school.

Often these conversations begin with questions about the nature of that language. I have been asked repeatedly, "Is Ebonics a language or a dialect?" I always seek clarification of what the questioner means by the term Ebonics. Although most people—including most linguists and most educators—have come to equate Ebonics with Black English or African American Vernacular English, presumptions of synonymy have not assuaged concerns about the status of Ebonics. I tend to agree with Labov's (1972) observations that American slave descendants speak English, but I am sympathetic to the Afrocentric observers who interpret Ebonics as being very distinctive. Indeed, some of my earliest research (Baugh 1980, 1983, 1984) confirms lingering traces of African grammatical influences and norms within contemporary speech patterns of American slave descendants. While I would be among the first to emphasize the unique linguistic consequences of the African slave trade on Black Americans and our posterity, I also recognize that African Americans have adopted a range of linguistic behaviors that conform closely to the vast majority of English grammatical and phonological rules. The noteworthy exceptions, however, are sufficient to maintain some of the lingering racial and linguistic stereotypes that I encounter among some teachers and student teachers who are willing to confide that they dislike nonstandard English and feel that African American students who do not invest in rapid development of Standard English proficiency are at a considerable social disadvantage, or worse—that they may be prohibited from access to abstract thought (Orr, 1987).

Challenges for the Future

Despite the controversy surrounding *The Content of Our Character* (Steele, 1990), the author has some contributions to make toward envisioning more linguistically adequate teacher education. Proponents saw Steele as being courageous for breaking with politically correct traditions advocating affirmative action for African Americans and other racially motivated preferential treatment that he finds abhorrent. Critics felt he pandered to majority public opinion through overt acts of hypocrisy in biting the very affirmative action hand that continued to serve him. But Steele's discussion of personal comfort zones was accurate and relevant to the future of teacher education and the welfare of low income and minority students. Briefly, he observed that most Americans are comfortable in the company of certain types of U.S. residents and quite uncomfortable with others. To his credit, Steele did not draw this distinction sharply along racial lines, although he does draw racial inferences when describing comfort zones.

I have found that many teachers and student teachers operate with their own variable comfort zones. On this point, I admire the young Teach For America volunteers who, perhaps naively, sign on to teach in some of the most difficult and challenging educational environments without regard to comfort zones. By contrast, several Stanford student teachers—most of whom share affluent backgrounds—have confided their relative discomfort at the prospect of teaching in the very kinds of schools where Teach For America volunteers routinely teach. Some experienced teachers have expressed similar observations, with the added dimension of having previously taught in inner-city and rural schools with limited resources and overcrowded classrooms.

Teacher education needs to come to terms with issues of teachers' feelings about their students. Most states regulate teacher education without substantial regard to student diversity and with even less regard to a student teacher's comfort zone with respect to teaching under circumstances where the majority of students come from backgrounds that are substantially different from those of the teacher. Parents, of course, hope that teachers who are teaching their children are comfortable with them and like them, but this hope may not be realistic given the preferences that we all bring to social interactions, professional or personal. Public school teachers cannot hand-pick their students. Teachers who are reluctant, resistant, or hostile to teaching low-income and minority students have no business teaching them and may, in fact, be in the wrong vocation altogether. Teacher preparation programs need to address this possibility head on.

My own reflections about the teachers I valued and disliked during my own education in inner-city public schools in Philadelphia and Los Angeles have helped me understand how profoundly teachers' attitudes affect their students' self-images and their achievement. My first-grade teacher, who was White, seemed neutral regarding her work with us; she did not seem to favor the few White students who were enrolled in the class. The second-grade teacher, also White, seemed favorably disposed toward teaching minority students; she conveyed her sense of pride in our accomplishments and she stimulated us to achieve. Our third-grade teacher was either resistant or hostile to teaching minority students or perhaps any student; she was ill-suited to the profession, and had I not had parents who were strong educational advocates I could have suffered greatly from her miseducation of our entire class.

We moved to California when I entered the fourth grade, where I encountered my first male teacher. He was White and favorably disposed to helping all students. I encountered my first—and only—African American teacher in the fifth grade. She was not only enthusiastic about teaching minority students, she was the most demanding of any teacher I had ever had. But her demands were not excessive; they were inspiring. She did more to encourage my academic advancement than any other teacher I have known. She also initiated conversations with my parents, rather than simply responding to them.

Shortly thereafter, my father and mother, both of whom were college graduates and successful professionals, moved to the upper-middle-class suburbs in the San Fernando Valley, where I became one of very few minority students in very affluent schools. It was in the context of "good schools" that I encountered the greatest racial hostility from some teachers and students who viewed my presence as a threat to their preconception that African Americans did not belong in their schools or the surrounding community.

As a linguist I have observed teachers and citizens who misunderstand the linguistic consequences of American slavery. As a teacher educator I have encountered teachers and student teachers who harbor negative stereotypes about Black students and who express their discomfort at the prospect of teaching minority students. As a minority student who attended both inner-city and affluent schools, I encountered a range of teachers and peers who were more or less comfortable with the prospect of helping Black students. This experience leads me to appeal to others to find ways to ensure that teachers and student teachers become effective with all students, regardless of their backgrounds, and to prevent educators who are reluctant or resistant to the prospect of teaching Black students from doing so in order to inflict no educational harm.

Because education still remains one of the best vehicles for peaceful social transformation through traditional values of hard work, delayed gratification, and personal reward, we cannot afford to squander the opportunities afforded to our neediest students by perpetuating failed policies or well-intended social experiments, ignoring potential teacher bigotry, or fielding unprofessional teachers whose effects on students are detrimental. To do so will not merely offer false hope to the student victims of unenlightened pedagogy; it will not prepare them to become the productive citizens that are essential to the well-being of a free, democratic republic that aspires to a national ethos of true equal opportunity and justice for all.

Notes

1. I wish to thank Carolyn Adger, Donna Christian, Margaret Reynolds, John Rickford, Geneva Smitherman, Orlando Taylor, and Walt Wolfram for their advice, suggestions, and continued support throughout the evolution and maturation of the Ebonics controversy. This discussion is based, in part, on research that has been funded by the Office of Educational Research and Improvement (OERI), U.S. Department of Education, in association with the National Center for Postsecondary Information (NCPI).

2. Again, Taylor's observations before the Senate are relevant. He made clear that some African Americans do not speak Standard English while others do (*Ebonics*, 1997). Educational policies that target the linguis-

tic behavior of Black students based on their race will be misguided at best, and detrimental to students at worst.

References

The Ann Arbor decision: Memorandum opinion and order & the educational plan. (n.d.). Arlington, VA: Center for Applied Linguistics. (ERIC Document Reproduction Service No. ED 273 140)

Baugh, J. (1980). "A re-examination of the Black English copula." In W. Labov (Ed.), *Locating language in space and time* (pp. 83-106). New York: Academic Press.

Baugh, J. (1983). *Black street speech: Its history, structure, and survival.* Austin: University of Texas Press.

Baugh, J. (1984). Steady: Progressive aspect in Black English. *American Speech, 50,* 3-12.

Bridges, E. (1992). *The incompetent teacher: Managerial responses.* Washington, DC: Falmer.

Brown v. Board of Education, 347 U.S. 483, 493 (1954).

Comer, J. (1997). *Waiting for a miracle: Why schools can't solve our problems—and how we can.* New York: Dutton.

Conference on College Composition and Communication. (1988). *The national language policy.* [Brochure]. Champaign-Urbana, IL: National Council of Teachers of English.

Darling-Hammond, L. (1994). Who will speak for the children? How "Teach for America" hurts urban schools and students. *Phi Delta Kappan, 76*(1), 21-34.

Ebonics: Hearing before the Subcommittee on Labor, Health and Human Services, and Education, of the Senate Committee on Appropriations, 105th Cong., 1st Sess. 68 (1997) (testimony of Orlando Taylor).

Farrell, T. (1983). IQ and standard English. *College Composition & Communication, 34,* 470-484.

Herrnstein, R., & Murray, C. (1994). *The bell curve: Intelligence and class structure in American life.* New York: Free Press.

Hollins, E. (1996). *Culture in school learning: Revealing the deep meaning.* Mahwah, NJ: Lawrence Erlbaum.

Labov, W. (1972). *Language in the inner-city: Studies in the Black English vernacular.* Philadelphia: University of Pennsylvania Press.

Ladson-Billings, G. (1994). *The dreamkeepers: Successful teachers of African American children.* San Francisco: Jossey-Bass.

Melnick, S. L., & Zeichner, K. M. (1997). Enhancing the capacity of teacher education institutions to address diversity issues. In J. E. King, E. R. Hollins, & W. C. Hayman (Eds.), *Preparing teachers for cultural diversity* (pp. 23-39). New York: Teachers College Press.

Orr, E. W. (1987). *Twice as less: The performance of black students in mathematics and science.* New York: Norton.

Rickford, J. (1997, December). Suite for ebony and phonics. *Discover: The World of Science,* 82-87.

Steele, S. (1990). *The content of our character.* New York: St. Martins.

Whiteman, M. F. (Ed.). (1980). *Reactions to Ann Arbor: Vernacular Black English and education.* Arlington, VA: Center for Applied Linguistics. (ERIC Document Reproduction Service No. ED 197 624)

Williams, R. (Ed.). (1975). *Ebonics: The true language of Black folks.* St. Louis: Robert Williams and Associates.

Chapter 6

The Case for Ebonics as Part of Exemplary Teacher Preparation

Terry Meier

In *Other People's Children*, Lisa Delpit reflects on the distance between the lives of many teachers and those of the African American children they teach:

> It has begun to dawn on me that many of the teachers of black children have their roots in other communities and do not often have the opportunity to hear the full range of their students' voices. I wonder how many of Philadelphia's teachers know that their black students are prolific and "fluent" writers of rap songs. I wonder how many teachers realize the verbal creativity and fluency black kids express everyday on the playgrounds of America as they devise new insults, new rope-jumping chants and new cheers. Even if they did hear them, would they relate them to language fluency? (Delpit, 1995, p.17)

In her study of language use in a Puerto Rican community, Ana Zentella takes her readers to New York's East Harlem to make a similar point about the distance between children's linguistic abilities and teachers' perceptions of those abilities. She describes the incredible facility with which members of the community can code-switch among the different language varieties that comprise their complex linguistic repertoires:

> Like basketball players who know where to hit the backboard in order to score a point, or salsa dancers who can follow a new partner's every turn, their interactions rely on shared linguistic and cultural knowledge of standard and non-standard Puerto Rican Spanish, Puerto Rican English, African American Vernacular English, Hispanized English, and standard NYC English, among other dialects. (Zentella, 1997, p.3)

The kinds of culturally specific speech events described by Delpit and the sophisticated code-switching abilities documented by Zentella are examples of ways of using language that are common to many bi- and multilingual communities in the United States, in which verbal performance and, in particular, the ability to adjust quickly and creatively to different audiences and purposes are both necessary and highly regarded linguistic abilities. Such abilities bear obvious connections to the development of effective writing skills and could easily be capitalized on in the classroom. They seldom are, however. Not in Philadelphia. Not in New York City. And not because teachers don't care about their students, but because most teachers don't even know these abilities exist. As Zentella writes, "Lack of knowledge about the socio-cultural context of code-switching, the grammatical rules it honors, and the discourse strategies it accomplishes . . . makes it impossible for educators to appreciate the bilingual skills of code switchers and to build upon them for the expansion of students' linguistic repertoires" (1997, p. 269). How can you build on a foundation that you don't know is there?

At Wheelock College in Boston, the mostly White, mainstream women who enroll in the graduate teaching program care passionately about children. Many have made major financial sacrifices to pursue a degree that promises few financial rewards. They come because they want to make a difference in children's lives. Yet most know little about the lives of children outside the mainstream or about the linguistic abilities they bring with them to school. And in many cases, neither do their cooperating teachers.

"The Only Problem Is They Don't Have Much Language"

At the first meeting, a student in my seminar talks enthusiastically about her current student teaching assignment in an urban, multicultural kindergarten. She really loves the children, she says. She tells us about "the little Haitian twins" who are "so darling." "The only problem is," my student says, her voice taking on a suddenly somber tone, "they don't have much language." We spend the next hour on the distinction between "not knowing English" and "not having language." The student recalls that the girls do talk animatedly with their mother in Haitian Creole when she picks them up after school. I end the class satisfied with a good discussion. Like the teachers Delpit describes, my student hasn't heard "the full range of [her] students' voices," but perhaps she now knows those voices exist. Leaving class, my student tells me (her defensiveness obvious, the slight challenge in her voice maybe my imagination) that it's her teacher who says the twins don't have much language and that's why they need a lot of extra attention.

I think of this interaction some weeks later when I am interviewing a woman to supervise student teachers. On her application, she has noted her fluency in Portuguese. She asks about supervising in a bilingual classroom. I tell her that we haven't had any students in Portuguese bilingual classrooms and mention our need for supervisors who can speak Cape Verdean Creole. "Cape Verdean Creole is not a language," the woman says.

Months later I think of these incidents again when I read an article describing a weekend-long tribute to the life and work of Jean-Claude Martineau, a Haitian poet who writes almost exclusively in Haitian Creole and who has struggled both in Haiti and the United States for official recognition of his native language. The author of the article quotes Martineau on what happens to Haitian Creole-speaking children in U.S. classrooms:

> Imagine an American child, about 6 years old, and he is going to school for the first time. . . . He does not go to school without a language. He has been climbing trees, throwing balls, playing with his father in the snow. The day he gets to school, the teacher tells him, "You speak no language. Everything you have learned to say—ball, tree, snow—is of no value." (Latour, 1997, p. B5)

I wonder how many readers simply assume that Martineau is exaggerating. Who could believe that teachers really do tell children that they have no language?

Some teachers really do. They tell this to Haitian children, to Cape Verdean children, and to African American children who speak Ebonics. Ebonics has been referred to as slang, street talk, home talk, sloppy speech, bad English, broken English, poor English, ungrammatical English. Sometimes teachers just say, "We don't talk *that way* in here," or "You can talk *like that* at home if you want to." These are all ways of delivering the same message: What you speak is not really a language. There are more subtle ways of delivering this message as well. Here is one.

99

"That's Not Right, Is It?"

I am observing a fourth-grade literature group made up of five girls who are among the lowest skilled readers in the class. In an effort to "motivate" the girls, all of whom are African American, the teacher has chosen Camille Yarborough's *The Shimmershine Queens* for the group to read. This appears to have been an excellent choice: The girls seem excited as they take turns reading aloud from their books. Then one of them comes to a section of dialogue in Ebonics. She hesitates and stumbles over the syntax. (Even though this child uses Ebonics features in her own speech, she is evidently not used to seeing them in print.) At that time the teacher says to the group: "That's not right, is it? That's not the correct grammar, but some people do talk like that." No one says anything, and the oral reading continues.

Later, when I ask the teacher about his comments, he is initially defensive. He thinks I am suggesting that he is not a good teacher, that he doesn't care about and respect the children in his class. I'm not. The truth is that in many respects he is an excellent teacher, and I know from observing in his classroom on numerous occasions how deeply he seems to care about his students. Like every responsible teacher, he wants his students to acquire fluency in the standard code. His negative comments about Ebonics, he says, grew out of fear that the girls would think "that kind of language is correct" or that "it's okay to talk like that." When I point out to him that a number of the African American children in his class use Ebonics features in their speech and that I've never heard him comment on their language, he says that the fact that he doesn't say anything doesn't mean he thinks their language is correct or "the right way to talk." There's something about seeing the language in print that underscores for him just how ungrammatical it is. His role is to teach his students "proper grammar," not to reinforce ways of speaking that will prevent them from getting ahead in life.

Clearly, this teacher does not think of Ebonics as a systematic, rule-governed language. In part, this is because his teacher preparation program did not require him to learn anything about linguistic diversity. I also suspect that he thinks of this language as incorrect because he has absorbed the prejudice of the larger society toward Ebonics. As a result, even though he cares deeply about his students and respects their feelings, it is difficult for him to recognize the inherent contradiction in using a book that enables children to powerfully identify with the characters and story line while simultaneously denigrating the language those characters speak.

It is this same linguistic prejudice and lack of knowledge that lead this teacher (and many others) to assume, falsely, that helping children acquire proficiency in Standard English requires "correcting" their Ebonics, rather than recognizing that each is a systematic language variety in its own right. Carrie Secret, a highly successful elementary school teacher in Oakland, California, speaks from 31 years of teaching experience when she says that as part of the process of developing fluency in Standard English, children who speak Ebonics need to develop an ear for both languages because they have to be able to distinguish between them (Secret, 1997). Obviously, teachers can't help children do that without possessing systematic knowledge about Ebonics. Yet because of the pervasive assumption that Ebonics is just an incorrect form of English, and therefore not worth serious study, teachers are unlikely to seek the very knowledge they need to help students acquire proficiency in the standard code.

In the multicultural children's literature course I teach, students frequently express discomfort about reading aloud texts written wholly or partially in Ebonics. This is a feeling shared by many teachers with whom I have discussed this issue. Not only do teachers feel uncomfortable reading the language aloud, but they are also unsure of how to talk with their students about Ebonics or about linguistic diversity in general. One teacher with whom I discussed Ebonics in children's literature spoke for many, I think, in expressing the view that White teachers shouldn't read Ebonics aloud for fear that African American children will assume the teacher is making fun of them. Notwithstanding this teacher's laudable concern with respecting children's feelings, her automatic assumption that Ebonics is something about which African American children (whether they speak it or not) are likely to feel embarrassed clearly reveals her negative view of it. When teachers simply avoid using children's literature with Ebonics, their students miss some of our most talented children's writers, including Lucille Clifton, Eloise Greenfield, Patricia McKissack, Walter Dean Myers, and Camille Yarborough. This is a major loss for all children, but particularly for African American children, who seldom have a chance to see their images and experiences reflected in the texts that are used in school.

"Noooo, Not Fifty Cent . . ."

Teachers' lack of knowledge about Ebonics features can result in misunderstandings that interfere with effective literacy instruction or that cause a child's abilities to be underestimated or assessed inappropriately. The classic examples are a child being needlessly "corrected" during oral reading for Ebonics pronunciations or a child being referred to a speech therapist because s/he doesn't pronounce consonant clusters the way the teacher does. Even when communicative misunderstandings don't lead directly to a negative outcome, they exact a heavy educational price by chipping away at children's belief that "what happens in school" and, in particular, "what the teacher says" can be counted on to make sense.

I am watching a student teacher working with a small group of first graders. They have finished their lesson and are playing with rhyming words. The mood is light-hearted, especially when one child offers the word *kiss* as a rhyme for *miss*. The mood changes abruptly, however, when another child calls out twis(t)," following the rules for consonant cluster reduction in Ebonics. "Twis? Twis?" asks the student teacher, clearly at a loss. She wrinkles her face in confusion. "What do you mean *twis*?" she asks, the heavy emphasis on "twis" making it sound like something repugnant. The child who called out his word with such enthusiasm and confidence says nothing.

As this student teacher's supervisor, I am able to intervene diplomatically and firmly. This is not the case on the day I observe a child answer "50 cent" during a math lesson. The teacher responds to this correct answer not with affirmation, but with a clumsy, and from the child's perspective, totally confusing attempt to teach Standard English grammar in a math lesson. "Noooo, not fifty cent . . ." the teacher says, her voice fading into a pause to which there is no response from the child who seconds before had been so sure that his answer was correct.

The phonological and grammatical rules a teacher would need to master in order to avoid these kinds of misunderstandings are relatively few. But this knowledge is neither part of the curriculum in the typical teacher preparation program nor likely to be pursued by individual teachers if they begin with the assumption that Ebonics-speaking children are simply making mistakes.

Beyond Phonology and Grammar

But Ebonics includes more than just phonological and grammatical features. Membership in any speech community entails knowledge of a wide range of communicative strategies for acting in the world—for demonstrating intelligence, apologizing, asking for a favor, telling someone what to do, claiming allegiance with others, displaying status, getting one's point across, even telling a story. As numerous studies of language socialization and use in African American communities suggest (e.g., Ball, 1992; Edwards, 1992; Gaunt, 1997; Goodwin, 1990; Hale-Benson, 1982; Heath, 1983; Labov, 1972; Morgan, 1994; Vernon-Feagans, 1996), by the time they enter kindergarten, African American children are likely to have formed a sense of identity and self-efficacy strongly linked to their ability to use language in highly sophisticated and stylized ways. In their communities, they are applauded for quick verbal responses, creative plays on words and sounds, imaginative improvisations of familiar stories and themes, and their ability to best an opponent through superior verbal reasoning.

Many African American children are used to participating in social situations such as Sunday school, church services, family gatherings, and community events in which language is highly interactive. In accordance with a characteristic communicative pattern called "call and response," African American preachers, politicians, storytellers, teachers, and plain old conversationalists expect their listeners to interject comments into the discourse. In the communicative tradition in which many Ebonics-speaking children are raised, sitting quietly while someone speaks is neither a sign of engagement nor of respect, as it is in the mainstream, Eurocentric communicative tradition. African American children enter school expecting to be active in discourse and to be praised for skillful use of language.

Because African American communities tend to value speaking well, children raised in these communities are also likely to have very high standards for what constitutes good verbal performance. They expect someone holding the floor to be engaging, rhetorically sophisticated, and elicitative of listener response. The ways that teachers use language do not always match children's expectations. Few schools of education emphasize developing skills in oral performance. Many teachers have grown up in communities that are not only geographically and culturally distant from those of their students, but less focused on oral performance and rhetorical style. As a result, African American children may be bored by their teachers' oral style and the lack of opportunities for active participation in classroom discourse. When this mismatch of communicative styles is coupled with the expectation that children will sit quietly even though they are bored, misbehavior of some sort is likely, and children are the likely target of blame. This is exactly what happens in the situation described below.

"Touch Your Fingers, Touch Your Toes . . ."

I am observing a first-grade "morning meeting," a time when children gather on the rug for calendar activities, sharing time, story reading, or some other special activity. The teacher has asked me to observe four African American children (there are 6 in this class of 18 children) who, according to the teacher, routinely engage in disruptive behaviors during meeting, such as calling out, talking with other children, hitting or poking classmates, and leaving the meeting area to play or stand in other parts of the room. On this morning, the student teacher is leading the meeting. I do indeed record numerous instances of inattentive or disruptive behavior by these four children. I also note the length of time during which children are expected to sit quietly while another child carries out a highly routinized, time-consuming task, such as searching for and attaching the correct felt numbers to the calendar or counting classmates to determine whether anyone is absent.

After the calendar activities, the student teacher reads *Lizzie's Invitation*, a story about a girl who does not receive an invitation to a birthday party. Although the reading is animated, the student teacher reads in a very soft voice, so any noise or other distraction makes it hard to hear her. She interrupts her reading several times because of the noise in the room. Twice she tells the class she will not continue reading until everyone is silent. Both times, however, she resumes reading while some children are still talking. After the reading, the student teacher invites children to share experiences of a time when they did not get invited to a party or when they felt left out in some way. Children called on for sharing remain in their places, and most speak so quietly that it is difficult to hear what they are saying. They all look at the student teacher when they speak. Again, the student teacher interrupts the activity several times to ask for silence. She does not solicit children's responses, but calls only on children whose hands are raised. None of the African American children raise their hands to speak. Near the end of the meeting, the student teacher leads an activity in which the children touch their fingers, toes, nose, and so forth to the accompaniment of a song playing on a tape recorder. Along with a few others, the four African American children I was asked to observe are totally disengaged.

To investigate the hypothesis that the four African American children who routinely misbehave (and perhaps others) are bored by the activities, the slow pace, and the limited opportunities for participation during morning meeting, the student teacher talks informally with individual children over the next week about meeting time. What she discovers is that a good number of them dislike morning meeting. Particularly memorable are responses from two of the African American children. One speaks with great disdain about the "baby songs" the teachers expect them to sing. When asked what he thinks about meeting time, another rolls his head from side to side and chants "la la la la la" in a sing-song voice.

Black Artful Teaching

In contrast, teachers who are highly effective in working with African American children (e.g., Foster, 1989, 1997; Hale-Benson, 1982; Hilliard, 1989; Hollins, 1982; Hollins, King, & Hayman 1994; Hoover, 1991; Irvine, 1990; Ladson-Billings, 1990, 1992, 1994, 1995; Piestrup, 1973; Secret, 1997; Smith, 1997) build on the children's cultural and linguistic resources. This is evident in the ways these teachers interact with children and structure opportunities for classroom participation, and in the kinds of texts, topics, and materials they utilize.

Teachers who are successful with African American students communicate excitement and passion about subject matter. They engage students' attention by using oral language effectively. Some use codeswitching for emphasis and dramatic effect. They use examples, analogies, and expressions relevant to students' lives. They handle themselves well verbally; they are able to think on their feet and to make a quick verbal comeback. They communicate appreciation of their students' facility with language and help them compare different forms and uses of language. They foster cooperation and collaboration among students and often utilize group participation strategies such as group recitation, choral reading, and call and response. They set a lively instructional pace. They are explicit in giving directions, managing behavior, and responding to students' work. They use culturally relevant texts and materials. They not only set high standards for all students, they also communicate their belief in students' ability to achieve those standards.

Many of these teacher characteristics and strategies are rooted in African American oral and literary traditions and depend for their implementation on the kinds of linguistic abilities and insights fostered through socialization in those traditions. This does not mean that teachers outside these traditions cannot acquire some of those abilities and insights or that non-African American teachers cannot be effective with African American children (Ladson-Billings, 1994). It is clear, however, that teachers unfamiliar with those traditions are extremely unlikely to inspire African American students to reach their highest potential.

" 'And This Old Lady Ain't Had No Sense' "

Without familiarity with students' traditions, how will teachers see them clearly? How will they recognize their strengths and envision their potential? Do most teachers recognize the sophistication inherent in Ebonics-speaking children's ability to code-switch? Delpit provides an example of an African American second grader whose teacher, in Delpit's estimation, probably did not:

> Second-grader Marti was reading a story she had written that began, "Once upon a time, there was an old lady, and this old lady ain't had no sense." The teacher interrupted her, "Marti, that sounds like the beginning of a wonderful story, but could you tell me how you would say it in Standard English?" Marti put her head down, thought for a minute, and said softly, "There was an old lady who didn't have any sense." Then Marti put her hand on her hip, raised her voice and said, "But this old lady ain't had *no* sense!" (Delpit, 1995, p.169)

As Delpit points out, this child is writing in the African American literary tradition of writers like Charles Chesnutt, Alice Walker, Paul Laurence Dunbar, and Zora Neal Hurston, whose rhetorical power is due in no small measure to their having made the same kinds of subtle and extremely sophisticated linguistic distinctions this child is making. Does it really matter whether this child's teacher recognizes her linguistic strengths? To answer that question, one need only contemplate the educational implications of a teacher viewing this child as a potential Alice Walker, as opposed to viewing her as a child who just can't seem to get it "right" the first time.

In a study of children's language socialization at home and at school, Vernon-Feagans (1996) speculates that the working-class African American kindergartners in her study may have performed less well on a paraphrasing task than their European American mainstream counterparts precisely because of their more creative use of language and their superior story-telling abilities (which she had documented in an earlier phase of the study). Instead of simply re-telling the story as most of the European American children did, the African American children embellished it, often creating a more interesting vignette than the original. However, because they had changed the story and left out details from the original, they were penalized on the paraphrasing task.

Research on language socialization and uses in African American communities (e.g., Ball, 1992; Edwards, 1992; Gaunt, 1997; Goodwin, 1990; Hale-Benson, 1982; Heath, 1983; Labov, 1972; Morgan, 1994; Vernon-Feagans, 1996) highlights linguistic strengths that Ebonics-speaking children are likely to acquire in their communities, including sophisticated story-telling abilities; skillful use of word play, rhyme, and rhythm; use of vivid metaphors and analogies; skill in indirection; the ability to think quickly on their feet; and facility in adjusting to different audiences. Clearly, these abilities provide a powerful foundation for literacy instruction. In fact, some of the language abilities that teachers struggle to help students acquire—the ability to interpret and manipulate metaphoric language, to read between the lines, to adjust one's language to different purposes and audiences, to infuse a sense of "voice" into one's writing and speaking—are the very abilities many African American children already possess in significant measure when they walk through the classroom door. The problem is that their teachers fail to recognize them.

"Long Before I Became a Writer, I Was a Listener"

In addition to contributing to the possibility of teachers underestimating or overlooking entirely the linguistic abilities of students, teachers' lack of knowledge about Ebonics and African American oral and literary traditions means they lack the knowledge base necessary to teach effectively in a multilingual, multicultural world. In the Author's Note that begins the delightful children's book, *Flossie and the Fox*, Patricia McKissack (1986) tells her young readers how and why she became a writer. In doing so, she expresses the important connection between oral and written language and suggests how intricately they are woven together in the experience of African American writers and orators:

> Long before I became a writer, I was a listener. On hot summer evenings our family sat on the porch and listened to my grandmother tell a hair-raising ghost story or watched my mother dramatize a Dunbar poem. But it was always a special treat when my grandfather took the stage. He was a master storyteller who charmed his audiences with humorous stories told in the rich and colorful dialect of the rural South. I never wanted to forget them. So it is through me that my family's storytelling legacy lives on.

Many African American writers and scholars have written with great eloquence about the important role that reading African American literature played in their own development as writers, as well as about the intimate connection between oral and written language in that development. In the passage below, for example, the literary scholar Henry Louis Gates, Jr. reflects on his adolescent discovery of James Baldwin's writings. Of particular significance here is his description of Baldwin's sentences and their connection to both oral and written traditions:

> Finding James Baldwin and writing him down at an Episcopal church camp during the Watts riots in 1965 (I was fifteen) probably determined the direction of my intellectual life more than any other single factor. I wrote and rewrote verbatim his elegantly framed

paragraphs, full of sentences that were somehow Henry Jamesian and King Jamesian, yet clothed in the cadences and figures of the spirituals. (Gates, 1990, p. 58)

The novelist Paule Marshall talks about how her writing draws simultaneously on the oral poetry—the sounds, metaphors, parables, and sayings—of her Barbadian mother and friends in their basement kitchen and on the written poetry and prose of Jane Austen, Paul Lawrence Dunbar, Henry Fielding, and James Weldon Johnson that she discovered in the Brooklyn Public Library (Marshall, 1983). Harlem Renaissance scholar Joyce Hope Scott recalls the lasting impact of an English teacher who gave voice to the written word in both Ebonics and Standard English:

> While I didn't think it remarkable at the time, I now find it fascinating that one of my most brilliant and articulate English teachers read Paul Laurence Dunbar's dialect poetry with a power and facility that I have not witnessed before or since. She could also bring an audience to its feet with her rendering of Edgar Allan Poe's "Annabel Lee" or Shakespeare's sonnet number twenty-nine: "When in disgrace with fortune and men's eyes/ I all alone beweep my outcast state." Even those with only minimal education could sense and understand the import of an "outcast state" and its relevance to them. To me, this teacher was magic and I wanted to be able, one day, to articulate with the artistry she possessed. (Scott, 1997, p.31)

The call and response pattern of oral communication in African American communities is put to literary use in Toni Morrison's novel *Beloved.* The oral "dozens" are refigured into the "thirteens" in a poem by Maya Angelou. The powerful cadences and mighty metaphors of Dr. Martin Luther King, Jr.'s sermons are echoed in his written masterpiece, "Letter from the Birmingham Jail." Great writers weave together in magical ways pieces of all of their linguistic experiences. For students to become powerful writers, they need teachers who can help them recognize the connections among diverse forms and ways of using language. The most essential connection for teachers to help children make in this regard is the one between oral and written language.

Oral and Written Connections

"Long before I was a writer, I was a listener," McKissack tells her readers. What is the relationship between these—the writing and the listening? How does the story she listened to her grandfather tell " 'bout lil' Flossie Finley" become transformed into text, preserving "the same rich and colorful language" that so charmed her in the telling? *Flossie and the Fox* is not written wholly in Ebonics. It combines Standard English and Ebonics in subtle and complex ways. In fact, the interplay between these two languages, as represented by the wily Standard-English-speaking fox and the witty Ebonics-speaking Flossie, lies at the center of the story. Flossie manages to outwit the Fox primarily because she is able to use language so much more effectively than he does. McKissack could not have written this delightful book had she traded in Ebonics as the price of her competence in Standard English. Nor could she have written it had she not believed that talk could be transformed into text, that what she heard could be written. She could not have written this book (nor, I believe, any other) had she lost faith in the power of her ear to guide her writing process.

For many years, I taught writing to community college students who had either never developed, or long ago lost, that faith. Among my students, most of whom were African Americans who spoke Ebonics, were some of the most consummate users of language that I have ever known. These were people who could hold the entire class spellbound while they recounted a hair-raising tale from their childhood or make us laugh until the tears streamed down our faces as they described, in exquisite detail, some hilarious scene they had observed on the bus that morning. Their lively commentaries on life and on the literature we were reading energized the class and pushed our thinking in new and provocative directions.

Yet as soon as these students—so full of ideas, fresh perspectives, penetrating insights—took pen in hand, their eloquence evaporated into tension-filled air. Despite their mastery of language, most could not write a narrative, essay, journal entry, or summary that came even remotely close to matching their oral sophistication. Why not? Not primarily because they lacked writing experience and certainly not because of their difficulties with Standard English grammar conventions, but because most had come to believe, through years of experience in school, that everything they knew about language (e.g., how to make a point, draw an analogy, create an image, tell a joke, move an audience, construct an argument, tell a story) had absolutely no relevance to writing as it was defined by their teachers. As a consequence, when they wrote, they didn't rely on their ear for language— their internalized sense of "what sounds good"—as they did when they spoke, when they made a point or drew an analogy in discussion.

My students may well have been as linguistically gifted, as full of literary promise, as James Baldwin, Toni Morrison, or Walter Mosley, but they were not as fortunate as these writers in finding someone who helped them discover the connection between the oral story and the Dunbar poem, between the language they heard all around them and the strategies of style—the subtle choice of word, metaphor, cadence—that move a reader to new insight and perceptions. For many African American writers, the people who helped them make those connections were family members—parents, grandparents, aunts, uncles, older siblings—or a respected elder in the community—a librarian, preacher, or exemplary teacher. In a society that ostensibly places so much faith in the power of schools to provide equal educational opportunity for all, we should be able to count on all of our teachers to help children make these connections between oral and written language, between the literacy tasks assigned in school and the language abilities children bring with them from their home communities.

Return to the Question . . .

Again, the question is, How can teachers help children make connections they themselves don't see? If teachers are unaware that an African American literary tradition even exists (let alone the importance of their having read extensively from this tradition), if they believe that African American children who speak Ebonics come to school speaking slang, how will they help empower those children to achieve their highest potential?

The underlying principle in all of this is that in order to make sense, new knowledge must be rooted in what children already know. The connection between the new and the familiar lies at the heart of learning. And yet we have the seeming contradiction that even though most teachers know little or nothing about Ebonics, the majority of children in our schools, including Ebonics-speaking children, do learn how to read and write. If Ebonics is such essential teacher knowledge, as I am arguing here, how does one account for that apparent contradiction?

In many cases, I believe, it is children themselves who make the essential connections between new knowledge and what they already know. If children were not so resourceful, if African American children in particular were not so alert to linguistic nuance, so skilled in reading social context, then we would have a great deal more school failure to account for than we already have. The reality is that many children become literate not because of, but in spite of, the instruction that occurs in our classrooms. In thinking about that majority of children who do become, to one degree or another, literate, there is also this to consider. There is a world of difference between simply being literate—able to read and write—and claiming literacy as one's own, a tool of empowerment, a vehicle for acting in the world.

If, in the absence of their teachers knowing the extent of their linguistic abilities, many Ebonics-speaking children have the inner resources to somehow survive in our schools, one can only imagine how they would shine if their teachers recognized their true abilities and knew how to build on their strengths. As I tell my bright, eager, committed-to-making-a difference students, they don't need to know anything about Ebonics to become teachers. They only need that knowledge if they want to become *great* teachers.

References

Ball, A. F. (1992). Cultural preference and the expository writing of African-American adolescents. *Written Communication, 9,* 501-532.

Delpit, L. (1995). *Other people's children: Cultural conflict in the classroom.* New York: The New Press.

Edwards, W. F. (1992). Sociolinguistic behavior in a Detroit inner-city black neighborhood. *Language in Society, 21*(1), 93-115.

Foster, M. (1989). It's cookin' now: A performance analysis of the speech events of a Black teacher in a urban community college. *Language in Society, 18*(1), 1-29.

Foster, M. (1997). *Black teachers on teaching.* New York: The New Press.

Gates, H. L., Jr. (1990). The master's pieces: On canon formation and the Afro-American tradition. In C. Moran & E. F. Penfield (Eds.), *Conversation: Contemporary critical theory and the teaching of literature* (pp. 55-75). Urbana, IL: National Council of Teachers of English.

Gaunt, K. D. (1997). Translating Double-Dutch to Hip-Hop: The musical vernacular of Black girls' play. In J. K. Adjaye & A. R. Andrews (Eds.), *Language, rhythm, & sound: Black popular cultures into the twenty-first century* (pp. 146-163). Pittsburgh: University of Pittsburgh Press.

Goodwin, M. H. (1990). *He-said-she-said: Talk as social organization among black children*. Bloomington: Indiana University Press.

Hale-Benson, J. (1982). *Black children: Their roots, culture and learning styles*. New York: Johns Hopkins University Press.

Heath, S. B. (1983). *Ways with words: Language, life, and work in communities and classrooms*. New York: Cambridge.

Hilliard, A. G. (1989). Teachers and cultural styles in a pluralistic society. *NEA Today*, 7(6), 65-69.

Hollins, E. R. (1982). The Marva Collins story revisited: Implications for regular classroom instruction. *Journal of Teacher Education, 33*(1), 37-40.

Hollins, E. R., King, J. E., & Hayman, W. C. (Eds.). (1994). *Teaching diverse populations: Formulating a knowledge base*. Albany, NY: State University of New York Press.

Hoover, M. (1991). Using the ethnography of African-American communications in teaching composition to bidialectal students. In M. E. McGroarty & C. J. Faltis (Eds.), *Languages in schools and societies: Policy and pedagogy* (pp. 465-485). Berlin: Walter de Gruyter.

Irvine, J. J. (1990). *Black students and school failure: Policies, practices, and prescriptions*. New York: Greenwood.

Labov, W. (1972). *Language in the inner city: Studies in Black English vernacular*. Philadelphia: University of Pennsylvania Press.

Ladson-Billings, G. (1990). Culturally relevant teaching: Effective instruction for black students. *The College Board Review, 155*, 20-25.

Ladson-Billings, G. (1992). Liberatory consequences of literacy: A case of culturally relevant instruction for African-American students. *Journal of Negro Education, 61*(3), 378-391.

Ladson-Billings, G. (1994). *The dreamkeepers: Successful teachers of African-American children*. San Francisco: Jossey-Bass.

Ladson-Billings, G. (1995). Toward a theory of culturally relevant pedagogy. *American Educational Research Journal, 32*(3), 465-491.

Latour, F. (1997, April 7). Poet sings of home so all of Haiti can hear. *Boston Globe*, pp. B1-B5.

Marshall, P. (1983). From the poets in the kitchen. *Reena and other stories*. New York: The Feminist Press.

McKissack, P. (1986). *Flossie and the Fox*. New York: Dial Books.

Morgan, M. (Ed.). (1994). *Language and the social construction of identity in creole situations*. Los Angeles: University of California Center for Afro-American Studies Publications.

Piestrup, A. M. (1973). *Black dialect interference and accommodation of reading instruction in first grade* (Monographs of the Language Behavior Research Laboratory No. 4). Berkeley: University of California.

Scott, J. H. (1997). Official language; Unofficial reality: Acquiring bilingual/bicultural fluency in a segregated southern community. *Rethinking Schools, 12*(1), 30-31.

Secret, C. (1997). Embracing Ebonics and teaching standard English. *Rethinking schools*, 12(1), 18-34.

Smith, B. J. (1997). Black English: Steppin up? Lookin back. *Rethinking Schools*, 12(1), 32-33.

Vernon-Feagans, L. (1996). *Children's talk in communities and classrooms*. Cambridge: Blackwell.

Zentella, A. C. (1997). *Growing up bilingual*. Malden, MA: Blackwell.

Chapter 7

Language Policy and Classroom Practices

Geneva Smitherman

The public debate on Ebonics that began in late 1996 and continues to this day spotlights the need for a national educational language policy. It is said that those who do not remember the past are doomed to repeat it. It is instructive, then, to review school language policies and practices so that policy making can proceed from this foundation. Here I quote from and comment on national and local policies relative to the language practices and educational success of African American students. Some of them continue to make sense. Those that never did are nonetheless instructive.

Foundations for Language Policy

One of the first scholars to confront the myth that African American speech is ill formed was the late Dr. Beryl Bailey, then at Hunter College in Black and Puerto Rican Studies. Referring to a discussion of "Negro" speech by H. L. Mencken (1937), Bailey (1965) wrote the following scholarly rebuttal:

> I would like to suggest that Southern Negro "dialect" differs from other Southern speech because its deep structure is different, having its origins as it undoubtedly does in some Proto-Creole grammatical structure. Hence, regardless of the surface resemblances to other dialects of English . . . we must look into the system itself for an explanation of [what Mencken had referred to as] the seeming confusion of persons and tenses. (p. 172)

Although Bailey's untimely death left much of her scholarly work unfinished, it was she who first re-raised the Turner-Herskovits 1940s question about the origin and uniqueness of the language of persons of African descent in the United States (see, e.g., Herskovits, 1941; Turner, 1949). Sista Beryl's paper (Bailey, 1965), from which I quoted here, was given at the 10th Annual Conference on Linguistics sponsored by the Linguistic Circle of New York, on March 14, 1965, when other scholarship was supporting the accuracy of her statements. It was subsequently published in *American Speech* (Bailey, 1965).

A little over a decade later, the well-known *King v. Ann Arbor* case of 1979 was brought by parents whose children were not learning to read (see *The Ann Arbor Decision,* n.d.; Whiteman, 1980). As an expert witness in that case, I presented evidence from school records of the failure to consider the children's dialect in teaching reading. I quote here from one of Judge Charles C. Joiner's early rulings in our favor:

> The . . . list of persons covered by [this language statute] . . . could well include students whose "language barrier" results from the use of some type of non-standard English. . . . The statutory language places no limitations on the character or source of the language barrier except that it must be serious enough to "impede equal participation by . . . students in . . . instructional programs." . . . [Thus] § 1703(f) applies to language barriers of appropriate severity encountered by students who speak "Black English" as well as to language barriers encountered by students who speak German. (*King v. Ann Arbor,* 1978, p. 1332)

At about the same time that language policy for Ann Arbor was being forged in Judge Joiner's courtroom, I argued in *Talkin and Testifyin: The Language of Black America* (Smitherman, 1977/1986) for a national policy that affirms the breadth of languages and dialects spoken in the United States:

> *Both* black and white students must be prepared for life in a multilinguistic, transnational world. [We] need to cultivate in students a . . . respect for . . . [and] celebration of linguistic-cultural differences . . . [and we need] to struggle for a national public policy on language which would reassert the legitimacy of languages other than English, and American dialects other than standard. (pp. 219, 240-41)

Next I quote, in its entirety, the *Students' Right to Their Own Language* resolution of the Conference on College Composition and Communication (CCCC), an NCTE-affiliate organization. The resolution was first passed by the CCCC Executive Committee in 1972, then reaffirmed by a vote of the membership at its annual business meeting in Anaheim, California, in 1974.

> We affirm the students' right to their own patterns and varieties of language—the dialects of their nurture or whatever dialects in which they find their own identity and style. Language scholars long ago denied that the myth of a standard American dialect has any validity. The claim that any one dialect is unacceptable amounts to an attempt of one social group to exert its dominance over another. Such a claim leads to false advice for speakers and writers, and immoral advice for humans. A nation proud of its diverse heritage and its cultural and racial variety will preserve its heritage of dialects. We affirm strongly that teachers must have the experiences and training that will enable them to respect diversity and uphold the right of students to their own language. (CCCC, 1974)

There are two major lessons to be learned from the past three decades of massive work on U.S. Ebonics. One is that we need a national multilingual policy, written into law, with full resources devoted to its implementation throughout the nation. The other lesson is that as far as language diversity and language attitudes are concerned, the school remains a critical agent of social change.

A National Language Policy

A national language policy that mandates multilingualism would not only advance the education of African American students; it would also advance the education of other students of Color and that of European American students. Being competent in more than one dialect or more than one language has at least three advantages: it sharpens cognitive skills; it prepares us to be citizens of our multilingual nation; and it prepares us to be citizens of the world.

Such a national language policy is already the organizational position of "the Cs" (to use the upscale, hip lingo of our younger colleagues in the CCCC). The Cs' *National Language Policy* (CCCC, 1991) is a progressive, evolutionary move forward from the 1972 students' right resolution, which was crafted primarily as a language policy for students on the margins who were speakers of nonstandard varieties of English. Adopted as an organizational position 10 years ago, *The National Language Policy* begins with a background state-

117

ment that recognizes the <u>need for a policy to prepare *everyone* in the United States for full participation in our multicultural nation.</u> Following is the full text of this policy, which was passed unanimously by both the Cs' Executive Committee and the membership at the annual business meeting in March 1988:

Background

The National Language Policy is a response to efforts to make English the "official" language of the United States. This policy recognizes the historical reality that, even though English has become the language of wider communication, we are a multilingual society. All people in a democratic society have the right to education, to employment, to social services, and to equal protection under the law. No one should be denied these or any civil rights because of linguistic differences. This policy would enable everyone to participate in the life of this multicultural nation by ensuring continued respect both for English, our common language, and for the many other languages that contribute to our rich cultural heritage.

CCCC National Language Policy

Be it resolved that CCCC members promote the National Language Policy adopted at the Executive Committee meeting on March 16, 1988. This policy has three inseparable parts:

1. To provide resources to enable native and nonnative speakers to achieve oral and literate competence in English, the language of wider communication.
2. To support programs that assert the legitimacy of native languages and dialects and ensure that proficiency in one's mother tongue will not be lost.
3. To foster the teaching of languages other than English so that native speakers of English can rediscover the language of their heritage or learn a second language.

Past School Language Policies

It is worth looking at some of the more infamous school language policies from the past. For example, back in 1917, the National Council of Teachers of English, then in its organizational infancy, led a national promotion of "Better Speech Week" (yes, the NCTE!). Recounting this history, Gawthrop (1965) writes:

This movement [for Better Speech Week] had originated in Montevallo, Alabama, the year before. It was patterned after "Better Babies Week," "Fashion Week," and similar festivities of the time. Its aim was to improve speech through such devices as posters, parades, newspaper articles, student elections of classmates who used the best speech, and short skits of the type in which "Mr. Dictionary" defeats the villain "ain't." . . . Better Speech Week became something of a national phenomenon for the next ten or twelve years with the NCTE serving as a clearing house. (p. 9)

One of the hallmarks of this national phenomenon was a pledge that students across the nation recited with regularity:

I love the United States of America. I love my country's flag. I love my country's language. I promise:

1. That I will not dishonor my country's speech by leaving off the last syllable of words.
2. That I will say a good American "yes" and "no" in place of an Indian grunt "um-hum" and "nup-um" or a foreign "ya" or "yeh" and "nope."
3. That I will do my best to improve American speech by avoiding loud, rough tones, by enunciating distinctly, and by speaking pleasantly, clearly, and sincerely.
4. That I will learn to articulate correctly as many words as possible during the year.

(quoted in Gawthrop, 1965, pp. 9-10)

The NCTE done come a long way, baby!

Over half a century after Better Speech Week swept the country, New York Public Schools Chancellor, the late Dr. Richard Green, teaming up with then-Mayor Edward Koch, focused on a list of 20 "speech demons." Green was dedicated to eliminating these demons from the speech of New York students. These are the 20 "demons possessing student tongues" (with the "demonic" phrase or word underlined):

May I axe a question?
Hang the pitcher on the wall.
He's goin home.
He be sick.

I ain't got none.

Can I leave the room?

I was like tired, you know?

Where is the ball at?

What-cha doin'?

I'll meetcha at the cau-nuh.

What do youse want?

Let's go to da center.

I brang my date along.

The books is in the liberry.

Yup, you betcha!

Pacifically . . .

I don't know nuttin about it.

I'm not the on'y one.

We was only foolin' 'round.

So I says to him . . .

(Lewis, 1989, p. 5B)

Although Mayor Koch hailed Green's plan as "superb," by this late hour in linguistic study, this linguistic demon eradication campaign failed the test of scientific scrutiny of language pedagogy.

Classroom Practices That Work

We have learned from the past that "better speech" pledges and linguistic exorcising do not work for *any* students, whether or not they are speakers of Ebonics. Clearly the school and classroom practices that *do* work for African American students are those that build on students' existing language resources and that teach from a linguistic philosophy of bi- or multilingualism. But in order for such a language pedagogy to thrive, two things need to happen: (1) Teachers need training in language diversity, and (2) classroom language practices must concentrate on the totality of the Ebonics world—what linguist Ana Celia Zentella (1997) calls a focus on not just the language in the community, but the community in the language.

The Ebonics community has a rich oral heritage. It is characterized by a fondness for and agility in verbal play, as evidenced in today's Hip Hop culture and Rap music. Twenty-first century language and literacy lessons should not only address the totality of language in life but should also allow for edu-tainment. I am sometimes awed by the innovative ideas coming from students in teacher preparation programs who take my "Language Use in the African American Community" course (not a requirement, by the way). Instead of a standard, written research project, they have the option of preparing materials for teaching about language. Some of their products include Ebonics Jeopardy, Ebonics Scrabble, Ebonics crossword puzzles, and activities involving African American proverbs. For the younger learners they include story books in Ebonics and coloring books with captions in Ebonics and the Language of Wider Communication. I have noted consistently that the students' products—with no prompting from me—involve translation exercises and have as their objective teaching language and literacy skills and teaching about both Ebonics and the Language of Wider Communication (and occasionally other languages as well). We need some research on the efficacy of such products in classrooms of African American learners.

By far the most concentrated and comprehensive classroom practices embracing a philosophy of multilingualism are those in Noma LeMoine's African American Language Immersion Program[1] in Los Angeles. Since 1991, LeMoine's program, designed for Grades K–8, has used a historical, linguistic, cultural approach, and a philosophy of additive bilingualism to teach language and literacy skills to students whose primary language is Ebonics. These materials have been field-tested in numerous schools in the Los Angeles Unified School District, and at last count, something like 25,000 students had been taught through this program (which is soon to be published as *English for Your Success*).

There are other classroom practices that exemplify the lessons we have learned from the past about effective language teaching for African American students. I mention three of them here.

In Detroit, right in the heart of the so-called inner-city, there are two elementary schools, both part of the Detroit Public School System, that are noteworthy for their work with Ebonics speakers and Latino students. At Malcolm X Academy, established in 1991 as an empowered—that is, site-based control—school, students have been taught Swahili, Spanish, and the Language of Wider Communication, all the while recognizing and legitimating the students' native Ebonics. (Unfortunately, this program has recently been placed in

121

jeopardy due to the intense budget crisis facing the Detroit School District. Both the Spanish and the Swahili language programs have been suspended—hopefully, only temporarily.) Results from the first assessment of Malcolm X Academy's effectiveness, done in 1994 by an independent evaluation agency, indicated that the Academy had more than met the Superintendent's criterion for continued self-governance, namely that within 3 years at least 75% of the students had to score at or above grade level on the California Achievement Test (Watson & Smitherman, 1996).

The other school is the Academy of the Americas, which has a two-way Spanish-English immersion program for its Latino and African American students. A formal systematic assessment is currently underway, but by anecdotal accounts it is a smashing success, both in teaching the African American students Spanish and in teaching the Latino students English—all the while reaffirming the legitimacy of each group's native language or dialect.

Finally, my study of Black student writing and teacher ratings of this writing in the National Assessment of Educational Progress (NAEP) concluded that there has been a shift in dialect sensitivity since the beginning of NAEP in 1969 (Smitherman, 1992). Aided by a research team comprised of writing teachers and one other linguist, I analyzed the writing and writing scores of Black 17-year-olds over a 20-year period, from 1969 to 1989. The writing samples consisted of nearly 3,000 essays written in the three National Assessments to date (1969, 1979, and 1988-89). The analysis focused on the presence or absence of syntactic patterns of Ebonics and the presence or absence of patterns of discourse typical of Ebonics speakers. By 1989, not only had the use of Ebonics syntax declined, but the NAEP teacher-raters were rating favorably essays that used Ebonics discourse features in lively, creative ways, despite features of Ebonics syntax that accompanied some of these essays. Furthermore, no longer were these teacher-raters giving high scores to essays that used Standard English but lacked content and style (Smitherman, 1994). I attribute this perspective of the NAEP teacher-raters to the efforts of groups such as the Center for Applied Linguistics, the Cs, and NCTE, which have provided leadership in calling for language awareness and language diversity training for public school teachers. This approach to literacy needs to be expanded.

I close with the words of South African President Nelson Mandela. In his autobiography, *Long Walk to Freedom*, he recounts a significant historical moment that perhaps foreshadowed what is now South Africa's national language policy, a policy of 11 official languages, now enshrined in that country's new democratic constitution. Mandela (1994) writes:

> I recall on one occasion meeting the queen regent of Basutoland, or what is now Lesotho . . . The queen took special notice of me and at one point addressed me directly, but spoke in Sesotho, a language in which I knew few words. Sesotho is the language of the Sotho people as well as the Tswana. . . . She looked at me with incredulity, and then said in English, "What kind of lawyer and leader will you be who cannot speak the language of your own people?" I had no response. The question embarrassed and sobered me; it made me realize my parochialism and just how unprepared I was for the task of serving my people. (pp. 96-97)

President Mandela's linguistic prescription of leadership poignantly captures the essence of what we have learned from our past struggles around language policy and classroom practices. The walk to linguistic freedom in the United States will not be over until we shed the myths and misconceptions about language that our implicit language policies and school practices continue to perpetuate.

Note

1. The African American Language Immersion Program has changed its name to Academic English Mastery Program.

References

The Ann Arbor decision: Memorandum opinion and order & the educational plan. (n.d.). Arlington, VA: Center for Applied Linguistics. (ERIC Document Reproduction Service No. ED 273 140)

Bailey, B. L. (1965). Toward a new perspective in Negro English dialectology. *American Speech, 40,* 171-77.

Conference on College Composition and Communication. (1974). Students' right to their own language [Special issue]. *College Composition and Communication, 25.*

Conference on College Composition and Communication. (1991). *The national language policy* [Brochure]. Urbana, IL: National Council of Teachers of English.

Gawthrop, B. (1965). 1911–1929. In R. McDavid, Jr. (Ed.), *An examination of the attitudes of the NCTE toward language* (pp. 7-15). Champaign-Urbana, IL: National Council of Teachers of English.

Herskovits, M. (1941). *Myth of the Negro past.* Boston: Beacon.

King v. Ann Arbor, 451 F. Supp. 1324 (E.D. Mich. 1978).

Lewis, N. A. (1989, February 28). Chancellor aims to purge "What-Cha's and Aint's." *New York Times*, p. 5B.

Mandela, N. (1994). *Long walk to freedom.* Randburg, South Africa: MacDonald Purnell.

Mencken, H. L. (1937). *The American language: An inquiry into the development of English in the United States.* New York: Knopf.

Smitherman, G. (1986). *Talkin and testifyin: The language of Black America.* Detroit: Wayne State University. (Original work published 1977)

Smitherman, G. (1992). Black English, diverging or converging? The view from the National Assessment of Educational Progress. *Language and Education, 6*(1), 47-61.

Smitherman, G. (1994). "The blacker the berry, the sweeter the juice": African American student writers and the National Assessment of Educational Progress. In A. H. Dyson & C. Genishi (Eds.), *The need for story: Cultural diversity in classroom and community* (pp. 80-101). Urbana, IL: National Council of Teachers of English.

Turner, L. D. (1949). *Africanisms in the Gullah dialect.* Chicago: University of Chicago Press.

Watson, C., & Smitherman, G. (1996). *Educating African American males: Detroit's Malcolm X Academy solution.* Chicago: Third World Press.

Whiteman, M. F. (Ed.). (1980). *Reactions to Ann Arbor: Vernacular Black English and education.* Arlington, VA: Center for Applied Linguistics. (ERIC Document Reproduction Service No. ED 197 624)

Zentella, A. C. (1997). *Growing up bilingual.* Malden, MA: Blackwell.

Chapter 8

Language, Diversity, and Assessment —Ideology, Professional Practice, and the Achievement Gap

Asa G. Hilliard, III

During the late seventies, when I was Dean of Education at San Francisco State University, I joined other deans in a meeting with linguists at the University of Pennsylvania. The meeting was sponsored by Dr. Dell Hymes. Its purpose was to brainstorm about the relationship of linguistic science to educational practice. As I recall, it was a very fruitful meeting. It meant a lot to me personally, because I had long been aware of the importance of language as a factor in mental measurement. However, I had not had the opportunity for in-depth discussion about these matters with linguists.

It was also interesting to me that although linguists, especially the sociolinguists and the linguistic anthropologists, had a rich expertise in linguistics, many had not explored in depth all of the ways language was tied to teaching and learning. Of course, this is not to say that some linguists had not been deeply involved in the education process. For example, Joan and Steven Baratz (Baratz, 1973) and Roger Shuy (Baratz & Shuy, 1969) were deeply involved in reading and linguistics as was Ken Goodman (Goodman & Burke, 1973) with his miscue analysis. Yet, as I reviewed the work of sociolinguists, it was clear to me that few were involved in a prominent area of education, that of assessment and mental measurement in particular. Assessment (finding meaning) is broader than measurement, yet it relies on measurement.

Linguistics and Education

Throughout my career, I have been deeply involved in measurement and assessment issues. It was evident to me from the start that linguistic understanding would be central to the development of validity in both testing and assessment. What was remarkable, however, was the reluctance of scholars and practitioners in the field of measurement and assessment to consider the contributions that linguistics could make to these psychological disciplines. The more I became informed about linguistics, the more clear I became about its vital importance in education and assessment and measurement. I have challenged my colleagues in psychology on this for many years, including Arthur Jensen (1980) on two occasions (Hilliard, 1984). I have tried to illuminate these issues in my research, at professional meetings, in my work in forensic psychology as an expert witness on test validity, and in my work on psychological assessment that is linked to instruction, especially in special education.

No matter where I have raised these issues, the response of colleagues in psychology has been minimal at best to the applicability of linguistic findings to psychological testing and assessment. This was true even though I was invited on several occasions to meet with senior staff of major testing organizations. Although I thought that my presentations were well received and in several instances stimulated excellent dialogue, it appeared to me that the consequences of an embrace of applied linguistics by psychometricians would fundamentally disrupt the practice of testing and assessment. Mental measurement experts fear linguistics and anthropological sciences, because they challenge the grounding assumption of universality.

The Ebonics controversy revealed just how deep the ignorance of professionals and the public is, in general, about matters of linguistics. In addition, the controversy demonstrated how propagandists could take advantage of this ignorance to demean the efforts of educators and the culture of parents and children. In fact, the controversy displayed on a grand scale the very thing that happens daily in schools on a smaller scale. We saw the ignorance and the virulent forms of degradation and disrespect that children encounter every day in regular classrooms, not only from people outside their ethnic group, but even by people who are members of their own ethnic group. To some extent, these attitudes prevail even among their own families. The Oakland Public Schools effort, although based on sound academic and professional footing, never had an opportunity to present its case. The negative mass media juggernaut led the rush to misjudgment. The roar of that rush drowned out the voices of those best able to render an evaluation, people who are specialists in the fields of cultural anthropology and sociolinguistics. The verdict of the Linguistic Society of America in support of Oakland was relegated to the back pages of newspapers and the public heard little or nothing of it.

A Manufactured Crisis

Very much disturbed over what they call the "manufactured crisis," Berliner and Biddle (1995) argue that a systematic propaganda effort directed at public education falsifies the record in order to destroy public education. They name people and institutions who produce falsified information to create the impression that the crisis in public education is much larger than it is, because they have a political agenda that would largely benefit the wealthy. I believe that many of the same propagandists created the media feeding frenzy against the Standard English proficiency program in the Oakland schools.

The fact is that in many instances the academic achievement gap between African and European Americans has been eliminated. Dr. Barbara Sizemore and I were chief consultants on a project called "Every Child Can Succeed" (Sizemore, Brosard, & Harrigan, 1982). We identified a number of public elementary schools where the children were in deep poverty but where their academic achievement was actually on the excellent end of the scale. In other words, whole schools defied the IQ predictions of low performance associated with low income and race. Instead, these schools were performing in the top quartile of achievement as measured by standardized tests. Some schools were at the very top of academic distribution, such as the Vann School and the Madison School, both in Pittsburgh (Backler & Eakin, 1993).

Some of the research on high-achieving schools is very interesting. For example, the West Virginia State Department of Education published a document called *Achieving Despite Diversity,* featuring schools that were successful in spite of low income and other diversity factors (Hughes, 1995). Perhaps one of the most astonishing reports in educational research was the Tennessee Value-Added Study by Sanders and Rivers (1996) from the University of Tennessee-Knoxville. They showed that children in third, fourth, and fifth grades who had three "good" teachers in a row scored approximately 50 percentile ranks higher on standardized tests than a control group of students who had a series of "poor" teachers. In other words, in both West Virginia and in Tennessee, as in our work with Every Child Can Succeed and other work, it is quite clear that quality of instruction alone accounts for a massive amount of achievement gains among children. The major issue in the achievement gap, then, is the distribution of the quality of teaching services. Clearly, it is not a matter of finding some special way to teach children who are considered to be disadvantaged. What the disadvantaged label really tells us is the low quality of instruction that will probably be made available to students from families that do not have wealth and power.

The Paradigm Problem

Much more could be said about the issue of the quality of instruction as the primary factor in producing an achievement gap. However, that is not my purpose here. Instead, I want to raise the issues associated with cultural anthropology and sociolinguistics and measurement and assessment. I have argued for many years that the primary problem in measurement or testing and assessment is the paradigm problem. The structure of the process, the type of questions asked, the purpose for the assessment, the definitions and assumptions are all critically important issues that may be illuminated by linguistic insights. I want to pinpoint just a few of the things that need to be done in the hope that an even broader examination by pedagogical and linguistic experts would yield even more points for consideration.

Linguists have been effectively shut out of the debate on measurement and assessment, even though some of them have written about these matters. It takes only a cursory review of the literature in measurement and evaluation texts, especially those that deal with the popular standardized measurement devices, to discover that the most relevant linguistic references are missing. It is interesting that Herrnstein and Murray's *The Bell Curve* (1994) attempted to demonstrate a sensitivity to linguistic scholarship. However, it is also clear that they picked over the linguistic data, leaving out the most powerful work of the best linguists (Hilliard, 1996, 1997). The expertise of linguists must be brought to the table. Linguists must be bold and courageous and demand to be heard for the simple reason that the enterprise of mental measurement and assessment is unscientific without their input.

Language Variation Issues in Measurement and Assessment

Teaching and learning are, at their core, a matter of communication; if anything, measurement and assessment are even more so. A look at the process of measurement and assessment as tied to teaching and learning shows examples of how linguistic work still has major contributions to make.

Measurement

Virtually all of the tools for mental measurement and achievement are constructed from language. Years ago, linguist Roger Shuy (1977) raised the fundamental question: Can we quantify linguistic data? Shuy's conclusion was that certain features of language, such as sound, might indeed be quantified. We might even count vocabulary. However, Shuy argued that the closer we get to the deepest structure of the language, its semantics and function, the less we would be able to quantify anything. Variation in rule-governed systems at the deep structural level prevents the standardization of instrumentation required by psychometry for mass production of instruments.

Gerald Zacharias, a physicist at the Massachusetts Institute of Technology, argued brilliantly about this matter of measurability (Zacharias, 1977). He ridiculed psychologists for applying the rules of measurement in physics and other hard sciences to data that do not meet the criteria for making a measurement instrument. Among other things, Zacharias pointed out that measurement required the construction of an *interval scale*, a virtually impossible task with language given the linguistic diversity in America.

During my 2 years on the Committee on Testing and Assessment of the American Psychological Association, I was unable to initiate a dialogue about this problem. If measurement is possible with linguistic data, certainly it is possible only within the context of linguistic commonality as far as standardized instrumentation is concerned.

Psychometric constructs

Test makers play fast and loose with certain terms representing fundamental constructs in psychometrics, such as *vocabulary*, *word difficulty*, *basic word lists*, and *reading level*. It is inconceivable to me that psychometricians producing standardized tests could claim to be working in an honest and valid way in the absence of the expertise that sociolinguists and cultural anthropologists bring to the discussion.

We are somewhat better in the case of language disorders and speech disorders. At least dialogue has gone into some detail over several years in the professional associations that deal with speech and language disorders (Van Keulen, Weddington, & DeBose, 1998). In spite of the gains in understanding among some measurement experts, however, the field has yet to hear of it broadly or to internalize it in ways that affect the masses of children.

Definitions of cognitive assessment

There is a need for the redefinition of cognitive assessment in light of our understanding of sociolinguistics and cultural and linguistic anthropology. Cognitive assessment is different from IQ assessment. In my opinion, IQ assessment is nothing more than a specialized form of achievement tests. Cognitive assessment, on the other hand, attempts to look at how human beings process information. This focus on the process as opposed to content calls for adding a very useful dimension to measurement and assessment. When the focus is on processes that involve communication, there is a vital need for linguists.

Language in measuring achievement

Little needs to be said about the requirement to determine the role that language plays in the measurement and evaluation of achievement. The makers of instruments for measuring achievement must disentangle children's achievement from variation in the language in which it is expressed. Linguists can help.

The multilingual reality

Overall the problem with all these issues and others as well is the implicit requirement that universal measurement instruments be constructed, even though the reality is that we have a multilingual world.

The Benefit of Testing

I was a member of the National Academy of Science's panel, *Placing Children in Special Education: A Strategy For Equity* (Heller, Holtzman, & Messick, (1982). That panel started out with a charge from the Office of Civil Rights to address the achievement gap between Black males and the mainstream population. Its charge was later changed to disproportionality in general. I was aware of the role of language in the assessment process and was instrumental in getting the criterion established for special education intervention and assessment—that assessment be shown to be beneficial for children before systems are implemented. In other words, the very act of assessment and the very instruments used must be shown to be a part of a larger effort that ultimately results in greater achievement gains for children. Otherwise, there is no need for them.

I would also argue that unless linguistics can yield added value, there is no reason for linguistics to become involved with assessment. I believe that for formal testing and assessment, and in fact for any other educational domain, the application of linguistics must be based on principles of benefit to students and professional practice and that applications to professional practice should be value-added. Applied linguistics has the capability for producing this benefit.

The Importance of Context

In other publications, I have pointed out that after many years of argument by some of us, including linguists, people have now begun to take into account the notion of context (Hilliard, 1976, 1983, 1984, 1987). The meaning to be attached to any responses given by children must take into account time, place, culture, and other contextual factors; otherwise there can be no comparability among the responses of students. This was the most important message of the International Think-Tank Conference on Intelligence and Measurement in 1988 (Rowe, 1991). It was also the central point in the farewell letter from the Editor of *The Journal of Educational Psychology* (Salomon, 1995).

Psychology has really been the slow learner with respect to the importance of context. I understand this failure: To acknowledge, accept, and take context into account creates a vastly more expensive process than one proceeding from a simple-minded assumption that all people are equally exposed to the same language, culture, and political and economic context. To acknowledge the importance of context is to require control for variation in context. That is the source of the additional expense. It would be better if this were not the case; however, the fact is that it is the case, and it must be considered.

The Context of the Ebonics Controversy

The poor treatment by so many people of those in the Oakland Public Schools who want to teach Standard English by acknowledging and responding to the context—the linguistic background of the students—displays ignorance and disrespect for African people. Even linguists who have studied the rule-governed nature of African American speech and language are often uninformed of the antecedents or source of the rules. To understand African rules means to understand African language, history, and culture. Only a handful of linguists understand this.

Africans have a multi-thousand year tradition of orature and literature. The slavery and colonial period effectively covered over information about these traditions, leaving many people with the belief that Africans function at a primitive level. Yet this orature and literature are the remnants of African languages that blended with American English and would explain the nature and source of the rules that vary from American English within African communities. Claudia Winfred Vass (1979) is one of the linguists who understands this. Perhaps the one who has brought the greatest genius to this analysis is Ernie Smith (1978, 1979).

Any honest examination of the African record reveals a profound respect for the *word,* perhaps above almost anything else. In ancient Nile Valley civilizations, the word is regarded as divine; in fact, their words for *word* contain their regard for its divine meaning. In the ancient Nile valley, "MDW NTR" or *word of god* was the name of the system of writing and the divine language spoken (Carruthers, 1995). *Nommo* (Jahn, 1961) is a West African generic reference to the word or more explicitly to the power of the word. *So* (Griaule & Dieterlen, 1986) is a Dogon (West African) word for *word.* In fact *Giri So, Benni So, Bolo So,* and *So Dayi* are levels of deep structure in the use of the word for Dogon people. One simply cannot know Africans and be ignorant of the power of the word, the respect for the word, the depth of the word that permeates everyday life in Africa.

The proficiency in the manipulation of language that is universal throughout the African continent can be found in such traditions as those of the local "linguists" whose role is to interpret the leader's message to the masses of the people; the "praise singer," whose role is to act as community historian and interpreter of experiences with appropriate editorial commentary—constructed and impromptu; and the ubiquitous proverbs that are used throughout the continent to convey deep ideas. The West African, Caribbean, and African American "rap" all testify to the profound proficiency in the manipulation of the word by people of African descent. Finally, we may mention the common role of Africans as linguists in the United States during the slavery period. Special mention of the linguistic capabilities of Africans as interpreters is made in such reference works as those that deal with the Maroon and Seminole populations in Florida and other parts of the country (Giddings, 1994).

The Ebonics controversy could not have occurred if we had been knowledgeable about the history of Africans and their languages in particular. It is a part of the context, the understanding of which is missing among educators. It is the source of some of the rich mother tongue of African people everywhere, including Oakland and New York. The obvious and desirable need for our children to learn the common language of the United States is not in question. Yet that in no way requires Ebonics bashing. In fact, it requires that competent professionals understand precisely what African American language is in cultural context.

My appeal is that we leave the periphery of the dialogue on measurement and assessment and move to the core, staking a claim on that part of the dialogue that linguists understand best. Measurement and assessment are, of necessity, multidisciplinary processes. The rules of the psychology guild to protect its members from competition by members of other guilds simply must be overcome if validity is to be infused into the measurement and assessment process and if that process is to be scientific. Linguists have the capability to deal with these matters. It is already late in the day.

References

Backler, A., & Eakin. S. (Eds.). (1993). *Every child can succeed: Readings for school improvement.* Bloomington, IN: Agency for Instructional Technology.

Baratz, J. (1973). The relationship of Black English to reading: Review of research. In J. Laffey & R. Shuy (Eds.), *Language differences: Do they interfere?* (pp. 101-113). Newark, NJ: International Reading Association.

Baratz, J. C., & Shuy, R. W. (1969). *Teaching black children to read.* Washington, DC: Center for Applied Linguistics.

Berliner, D. C., & Biddle, B. J. (1995). *The manufactured crisis: Myth, fraud and the attack on America's public schools.* New York: Addison-Wesley.

Carruthers, J. (1995). *MDW NTR: Divine speech, a historical reflection of African deep thought from the time of the pharaohs to the present.* London: Karnak House.

Giddings, J. (1994). *The exiles of Florida: Or the crimes committed by our government against the maroons who fled from South Carolina and other slave states seeking protection under Spanish laws 1858.* Baltimore, MD: Black Classics.

Goodman, K., & Burke, C. (1973). *Theoretically based studies of patterns of miscues in oral reading performance* (U.S.O.C. Project No. 90375, Grant No. OEG-0-9-320375-4269). Washington, DC: U. S. Department of Health, Education and Welfare.

Griaule, M., & Dieterlen, G. (1986). *The pale fox.* Chino Valley: Arizona Continuum Foundation. (Available: P. O. Box 636, Chino Valley, AZ 86322)

Heller, K. A., Holtzman, W. H., & Messick, S. (1982). *Placing children in special education: A strategy for equity.* Washington, DC: National Academy Press.

Herrnstein, R., & Murray, C. (1994). *The bell curve: Intelligence and class structure in American life.* New York: Free Press.

Hilliard, A. G., III. (1976). *Alternatives to IQ testing: An approach to the identification of gifted "minority" children* (Final report to the California State Department of Education, Special Education Support Unit). (ERIC Document Reproduction Service No. ED 146 009)

Hilliard, A. G., III. (1983). Psychological factors associated with language in the education of the African American child. *Journal of Negro Education, 52,* 24-34.

Hilliard, A. G., III. (1984). I.Q. testing as the emperor's new clothes: A critique of bias in mental testing. In C. Reynolds & R. E. Brown (Eds.), *Perspective on bias in mental testing*. New York: Plenum.

Hilliard, A. G., III. (Ed.). (1987). Testing African American students. *Negro Educational Review, 38*, 2-3.

Hilliard, A. G., III. (1996). Either a paradigm shift or no mental measurement: The non-science and nonsense of the bell curve. *Cultural Diversity and Mental Health Journal, 2*, 1-20.

Hilliard, G. G., III. (1997). Language, culture, and the assessment of African American children. In A. L. Goodwin (Ed.), *Assessment for equity and inclusion: Embracing all our children* (pp. 229-238). New York: Routledge.

Hughes, M. F. (1995). *Achieving despite adversity: Why are some schools successful in spite of the obstacles they face? A study of the characteristics of effective and less effective elementary schools in West Virginia using qualitative and quantitative methods*. Charleston, WV: West Virginia Education Fund.

Jahn, J. (1961). *Muntu: The new African culture*. New York: Grove.

Jensen, A. (1980). *Bias in mental testing*. New York: Free Press.

Rowe, H. A. H. (Ed.). (1991). *Intelligence reconceptualization and measurement*. Hillsdale, NJ: Lawrence Erlbaum.

Salomon, G. (1995). Reflections on the field of educational psychology by the outgoing journal editor. *Educational Psychologist, 30*, 105-108.

Sanders, W. L., & Rivers, J. C. (1996). *Cumulative and residual effects of teachers on future student academic achievement: Value added research and assessment*. Knoxville, TN: University of Tennessee.

Shuy, R. (1977). Quantitative linguistic analysis: A case for and some warnings against. *Anthropology and Education Quarterly, 1*, 78-82.

Sizemore, B., Brosard, C., & Harrigan, B. (1982). *An abashing anomaly: The high achieving predominately Black elementary schools*. Pittsburgh: University of Pittsburgh Press.

Smith, E. A. (1978). *The retention of the phonological, phonemic, and morphophonemic features of Africa in Afro-American Ebonics* (Seminar paper No. 40). Fullerton, CA: California State University-Fullerton, Department of Linguistics.

Smith, E. A. (1979). *A diagnostic instrument for assessing phonological competence and performance of the inner-city Afro-American child* (Seminar paper No. 41). Fullerton, CA: California State University-Fullerton, Department of Linguistics.

Van Keulen, J., Weddington, G. T., & DeBose, C. E. (1998). *Speech, language, learning and the African American child.* Needham Heights: Allen.

Vass, Claudia W. (1979). *The Bantu speaking heritage of the United States.* Los Angeles, CA: Center for Afro-American Studies.

Zacharias, J. R. (1977). The trouble with tests. In P. L. Houts (Ed.), *The myth of measurability* (pp. 69-70). New York: Hart.

Chapter 9

Lessons Learned
From the Ebonics Controversy—
Implications for Language Assessment

Anna F. Vaughn-Cooke

Introduction

For a brief period at the end of 1996 and the beginning of 1997, an unprecedented number of people in the United States engaged in an impassioned and often acrimonious debate about a specific variety of English—Ebonics. The intense and sometimes heated discussions attracted nearly everyone: the young, the old, Whites, Blacks, teachers, preachers, poets, politicians, leaders, followers, and, predictably, language professionals—linguists and speech-language pathologists (SLPs). The debate provided an important opportunity for SLPs to refocus on a longstanding professional challenge: providing valid language assessments for speakers of Ebonics, or African American Vernacular English (AAVE).

Given the knowledge about Ebonics from several decades of impressive, convincing linguistic research, it is safe to say that practitioners have more than enough information to provide an adequate assessment of the language of African American children. We already know a lot about their phonological, syntactic, semantic, and pragmatic systems (although we can always learn more). In other words, we already know enough to determine whether an African American child's language is normal.

Why, then, are so many invalid assessments still being made and used to place African American children in special education and related services? During the Ebonics debate the Oakland Unified School District reported that a staggering 71% of the students enrolled in special education were African American. This figure suggests that professionals did not learn anything from the Black English trial that focused on 11 Ebonics-speaking children at the Martin Luther King, Jr. Elementary School in Ann Arbor, Michigan (Smitherman 1981), where the children were placed in special education classes after language assessments failed to take into account their linguistic heritage. Judge Joiner ordered the Ann Arbor School

District to take linguistic differences into account when teaching academic subjects like reading and language arts.

While valid assessment for Ebonics speakers is still a major challenge for speech-language pathology, an even more formidable challenge facing the profession and the educational system is the *American people's assessment* of the language of Ebonics speakers. The Ebonics debate revealed that a linguistically naïve public considers that Ebonics is inferior and unfit for classroom use, and that the children who speak it have limited intelligence. When we consider that regular and special education teachers and other professionals who provide basic services for Ebonics speakers come from the ranks of the American people who share this general perspective, we should not be surprised that so many African Americans are placed in special education and related services.

A first step toward solving the problems caused by the public's overwhelmingly contemptuous assessment of Ebonics is to study critically some of the lessons learned from the debate. They reveal that our 30-year-old strategy of simply restating the well-researched linguistic facts about the dialect needs to be abandoned, because it has not worked. I propose a new strategy, one that includes a national language policy supported by legislation (Baugh, 1998). I will first discuss the lessons learned from the Ebonics debate, then my proposed strategy.

Lesson #1—The majority of people in the United States do not believe that all languages are equal.

In spite of the fact that linguists have provided substantial evidence that all languages are equal in their capacity to serve as communication systems, we learned during the debate that the ill-founded belief that some languages are better than others is deeply entrenched in the minds of millions of Americans. People do not believe that rating some languages as good and others as bad is completely arbitrary, as Stanford linguist, Merritt Ruhlen, demonstrates with a hypothetical reversal of the historical record:

> If history had gone differently and Africans had come over and founded America and raided Europe and brought white slaves over, and this country ended up with a 10 percent white minority that

was kept in ghettos and spoke white English, you'd find the same problems in reverse . . . People would be saying, "Why can't the whites learn good black English?" We spend all of our time in school learning "good" and "bad" grammar and can't see that it's an historical accident that white English is called the best. (Weiss, 1997, p. A10)

Irrational beliefs about the quality of languages cannot be changed by energetic presentations of linguistic facts. Language professionals and others who are committed to helping Ebonics speakers resist the social, educational, and economic subordination caused by irrational views about the quality of their language should develop new strategies that focus on changing national language policies (particularly those related to education) and not the minds of the majority.

Lesson #2—The majority of people believe that Ebonics and other nonstandard varieties of English are deficient.

While language professionals, particularly SLPs and linguists, have argued for decades that Ebonics is *different* from Standard English, but not deficient, the debate taught us that the majority of people in the United States believe that Ebonics is inferior. This was evidenced by a proliferation of derogatory terms used to characterize the dialect. "You can call it Ebonics, but we call it junk" (Bowman, 1997, p. C5) said Patricia Chase, chairman of the English Department at Roosevelt Senior High School in Washington, D.C. Mary McGrory, a *Washington Post* columnist, maintained that the Oakland School Board was "legitimizing gibberish" (McGrory, 1996). Other writers used a disease metaphor as titles of their articles: A column in the *Economist* was entitled "The Ebonics Virus"; the *Wall Street Journal* published a column called "The Ebonic Plague" (Rich, 1997); *San Francisco Examiner's* Rob Morse (1997) entitled his column, "1996: E. coli, Odwalla, ebola, ebonics." Finally, Herb Boyd (1997) in his *Black Scholar* article, "Been dere, done dat!" said, "The Ebonics debate swept the nation like a verbal ebola plague."

The linguistic facts about Ebonics have been resoundingly rejected by some of the most respected leaders and politically astute members of the larger African American community. If the American people are listening to linguists on this point, they are certainly not agreeing with them.

Lesson #3—Many people believe that Ebonics is only slang.

"The Clinton administration declared that . . . 'black English' is a form of slang that does not belong in the classroom," reported John F. Harris (1996), a staff writer for the *Washington Post*. The administration presumably made this claim without consulting the language professionals who have been awarded millions of federal dollars to conduct research that proves that Ebonics is not slang. Slang, according to Smitherman (1997), "refers to forms of speech that are highly transitory and limited to specific sub-groups, e.g., today's Hip Hoppers" (p. 29). Ebonics and all other dialects of English, including Standard English (SE), have slang words and phrases; these usually constitute only a fraction of the linguistic knowledge required to speak and comprehend a language. The claim that Ebonics speakers use only slang is blatantly false.

The view that Ebonics is slang was supported by the syndicated columnist Carl Rowan (1996), who said, "Telling youngsters that a slang called black English (dressed up as 'Ebonics') is good enough for them . . . is guaranteeing failure for all youngsters who swallow this copout from hard work and study." The *New York Times* also disseminated the slang falsehood. An editorial stated that "the school board in Oakland . . . blundered badly . . . when it declared that black slang is a distinct language that warrants a place of respect in the classroom" ("Linguistic Confusion," 1996).

The relegation of Ebonics to the linguistically trivial category of slang, without consulting any of the language experts, provides evidence that the American people, including the most powerful leaders in the country, have no intention of changing their negative assessments of Ebonics.

Lesson #4—Many people believe that Ebonics is street language.

"After years of dumbing down the curriculum . . . are we about to rule that street slang is a distinct language deserving of respect?" asked Mona Charen (1997, p. A7) in the *Detroit News*. Columnist George F. Will (1997) called Ebonics "the patois of America's meanest streets" (p. B12), and a *New York Times* editorial noted that "the new policy is intended to help teach standard English and other subjects by building on the street language actually used by many inner-city children and their parents" ("Linguistic Confusion," 1996, p. A10). Eldridge Cleaver (1997) summed up his position about Ebonics this way: "The only place for Ebonics is the streets. We don't need it in the classroom" (p. A36).

Cast aside here is the linguistic insight that no dialect, or variety of language, is spoken only in the street. The journalist Mumia Abu-Jamal (1997) emphasizes that Ebonics, "for millions of us in the inner cities, and in the projects, is not street language—but home language, where we communicate our deepest feelings, fears, views and insights" (p. 27). Ebonics is spoken in homes where it is often the preferred dialect; it is spoken in many churches and numerous other places, including schools all over the United States. Indeed, it was the use of Ebonics in the Oakland schools that motivated the Board to draft the resolution that sparked the debate. The controversy revealed that many children in the United States are made to feel ashamed of the way that they speak everyday, because their English is reviled as street language.

Lesson #5—Many people believe that Ebonics speakers have limited intelligence.

The intelligence of Ebonics speakers was frequently maligned during the debate; this was especially evident in some of the vicious material on the Internet. The example below is illustrative.

Subject: Ebonics 101

Leroy Washington is an (sic) 19 year old third grader in the city of Oakland who is becoming increasingly disillusioned with the public school system. One day Leroy got an easy homework assignment.

> All he had to do was put each of the following words in a sentence. This is what Leroy did.
>
> HOTEL—I gave my girlfriend da crabs and the HOTEL everybody.
>
> DISAPPOINTMENT—My parole officer tol me if I miss DISAPPOINT-MENT they gonna send me back to the big house.
>
> UNDERMINE—There is a fine lookin' hoe livin' in the apartment UNDERMINE.
>
> [http://www.tcnet.net/joe/ebonics.html]

These are 3 of the 15 sentences created by someone with an exceptionally high level of metalinguistic awareness. The fact that the person chose to use his or her special skills to launch such a blatant and cruel attack on the intelligence and moral character of students in the Oakland school system is chilling.

Jokes about the supposed low intelligence of Ebonics speakers were common during the debate. These jokes proliferated despite the fact that Bill Cosby and many others who ridiculed Ebonics probably know numerous intelligent people who speak the dialect. For example, the civil rights activist, brilliant strategist, and organizer, Fannie Lou Hamer, spoke Ebonics, and she was not ashamed of her dialect. In 1964, Ms. Hamer led 68 delegates of the Mississippi Freedom Democrats, a party that she helped to organize, to the Democratic National Convention in Atlantic City. The following is an excerpt from the speech she gave there.

> Senator Humphrey, I ain't no stranger to struggle . . . It was a struggle to get 68 of us here as delegates from the cotton fields of Mississippi . . . to the National Democrat convention, but we kept a struggling and we made it here. And we is asking you to help . . . Senator Humphrey, you can help us in this struggle if you want to; you just got to get up your nerve and go in there and do it! (Young, 1991, p. 525)

The following portion of Ms. Hamer's speech was directed to Roy Wilkins, then head of the NAACP.

> Mr. Wilkins, I know that you is a good spokesperson for the Negro peoples, and for the NAACP: I'm is not a sophisticated politician is

you. And I know that you can speak clearer than me . . . sometimes. But you know Mr. Wilkins, I ain't never seed you in my community in Missippi, and them is the people I represents, them is the people I speaks for. And they done already told me that we didn't come all this'a way for no two seats, since all a' us is tired. (Young, 1991, p. 525)

Ms. Hamer's extraordinary level of intelligence was acknowledged by a number of institutions of higher learning, as evidenced in an acceptance speech she made at Morehouse College.

To the president of Morehouse College . . . I want to thank you for inviting me here. I have just left Tougaloo College where this morning I received a honorary Doctorate of Humane Letters; and I am on my way to Howard University where I expect to receive another honorary Doctorate of Humane Letters. And I wants to thank you Morehouse, for this Plaque. (Young, 1991, p. 526)

To make fun of the way the Fannie Lou Hamers of the world speak is a conscious and cruel tactic employed to make Ebonics speakers feel intellectually inferior and ashamed of the way they speak. Labov (1972) spoke out against such tactics more than 25 years ago.

Teachers are now being told to ignore the language of Black children as unworthy of attention and useless for learning. They are being taught to hear every natural utterance of the child as evidence of his mental inferiority. As linguists we are unanimous in condemning this view as bad observation, bad theory, and bad practice. (p. 67)

The stunning insensitivity of many of the views expressed during the Ebonics debate demonstrates that Labov's words went largely unheeded.

Lesson #6—Many people believe that listeners cannot understand Ebonics.

"I think it's tragic . . . These are kids [who] have gotten themselves into this trap of speaking this language—this slang, really—that people can't understand. Now we are going to legitimize it" (Sneider, 1996, p. 1) Thus Ward Connerly, an African American businessman and University of California regent, summed up his reaction to the Oakland resolution. Like many other Americans, Connerly claims that Ebonics is difficult to understand. This myth was perpetuated by Bill Cosby (1997) in his parody of Ebonics that appeared in the *Wall Street Journal*.

> The first thing people ask when they are pulled over [by a policeman] is: "Why did you stop me officer?" Imagine an Ebonics-speaking Oakland teenager being stopped on the freeway by a non-Ebonics speaking California Highway Patrol officer. The teenager, posing that same question Ebonically, would begin by saying: "Lemme ax you . . . " The patrolman, fearing he is about to be hacked to death, could charge the kid with threatening a police officer. Thus, to avoid misunderstandings, notices would have to be added to driver's licenses warning: "This driver speaks Ebonics only."

But Patricia J. Williams (1996), who is not a linguist, made a further point about the comprehensibility of Ebonics.

> Perhaps the real argument is not about whether ebonics is a language or not. Rather, the tension is revealed in the contradiction of black speech being simultaneously understood yet not understood. Why is it so overwhelmingly, even colorfully comprehensible in some contexts, particularly in sports and entertainment, yet deemed so utterly incapable of effective communication when it comes to finding a job as a construction worker? (section 4, p. 9)

As Williams suggests, the real issue is not the listener's ability to understand Ebonics, but the listener's objection to persons speaking Ebonics. Exceptions are always made, however, for certain words and phrases that exemplify the coveted linguistic creativity of Ebonics speakers. These are of course quickly appropriated by the mainstream. Consider the following verse from a poem used by Nike in a *Black Enterprise Magazine* advertisement (September 1997) featuring the golfer Tiger Woods:

> You the Man, Mr. Rhodes.
> You the Man, Mr. Sifford.
> You the Man, Mr. Elder.
> I won't forget.

The familiar Nike logo appeared in bold relief at the end of the poem.

"You the man" is a distinct creation of Ebonics speakers; it means something like "you are the person with the power and I respect you." Note the absence of the copula verb "are," a common syntactic pattern in Ebonics. The moguls at Nike had no difficulty understanding "You the man."

Another Ebonics expression that has been appropriated by the mainstream is "You go, girl," a phrase used to refer to a female who has completed an act of triumph, or who is about to engage in an act that is expected to end triumphantly. The February 23, 1998, cover of *People Magazine* featured the White American skaters Tara Lipinski and Nicole Bobeck and the Asian American Michele Kwan just before their Olympic competitions. Juxtaposed to the pictures, in big, bold letters, was Ebonics: "You go, girls!" Comprehension was not a problem for *People Magazine* or its readers.

During the Ebonics debate, a number of linguistically astute writers commented on the appropriation phenomenon. One was the African American columnist Michael Datcher. He said, "If the millions of white Americans who buy hip hop music teach us anything, it is that white people love the way we turn a phrase" (1997, p. 15). This phenomenon is never acknowledged by the mainstream, as Dr. Mahmoud El-Kati, a history professor at Macalester College in Minnesota, pointed out in his analysis of the Ebonics controversy:

> There is a darker side to . . . this appropriation . . . that has to do
> with power and the ability to wield it . . . In a sense, black English
> is elevated when it is incorporated in the wider culture . . . but
> when it comes out of black people's mouths it is associated with
> degradation or stupidity." (DeWitt, 1996, section 4, p. 3)

In sum, Fannie Lou Hamer's speeches (she made many of them all over the country) and examples of appropriation by non-Ebonics speakers debunk the tired old myth that Ebonics is incomprehensible. There is abundant evidence that mainstream speakers not only understand Ebonics, they often borrow words and phrases from it, especially when these borrowings are economically and socially beneficial. However, many mainstream speakers need to justify their rejection and denigration of Ebonics; they do this by claiming that the dialect is incomprehensible. Arguing linguistic facts with such people is futile.

Lesson #7—The evidence that Ebonics is systematic and rule-governed is often rejected or ignored.

During the Ebonics debate, a simple but fundamental fact about Ebonics—that it is systematic and rule-governed like all languages of the world—was repeated on national and local television and on radio shows and in the print media by some of the most respected linguistic scholars and language specialists in the world. Yet a startling number of highly educated, intelligent, and talented people with a high level of awareness about language refused to accept this fact. The syndicated columnist William Raspberry was one of them. In a satirical column on Ebonics entitled, "To Throw in a Lot of 'Bes,' or Not? A Conversation on Ebonics," one of Raspberry's characters, a cab driver, concluded that it was not necessary for Ebonics speakers to follow linguistic rules:

> "Just out of curiosity, who corrects your Ebonics?"
>
> "That's the beautiful part," the cabbie said. "Ebonics gives you a whole range of options. You can say 'she wish' or 'they goes,' and it's all perfectly fine. But you can also say 'they go,' and that's all right, too. I don't think you can say 'I does.' I'll have to check on that, but my brother-in-law tells me *you can say pretty much what you please, as long as you're careful to throw in a lot of 'bes' and leave off final consonants.'* " (emphasis added) (Raspberry, 1996, p. A27)

The cab driver's conclusion, in italics above, is patently false. There is no language in the world in which speakers can say "pretty much" what they please: The absence of rules would make it impossible for speakers to communicate with each other. The use of "be" in Ebonics is governed by a set of semantic-syntactic rules that must be followed in order to use the form correctly. However, Raspberry seems to believe that Ebonics speakers are incapable of linguistic complexity. Perhaps that is why some of his examples of the use of habitual "be" were incorrect; for example the last sentence in the column —'Yo!' " I said. 'Maybe you be onto somethin' dere, my bruvah' "— exhibits an incorrect use of habitual "be." The form is never used to refer to the present; it is used to refer only to actions that occur habitually over time, for example, "Ricky be playing in the yard." This sentence expresses the concept that Ricky usually engages in playing in the yard. Raspberry's character should have said, "Maybe you onto somethin' dere, my bruvah"; the inflected form of "be" ("are") can be absent in this sentence.

Geoffrey Pullum, a professor of linguistics at the University of California, Santa Cruz, wrote a long and detailed letter to Raspberry, pointing out where the language of the characters in his column violated the linguistic rules of Ebonics. He ended his letter by saying this:

> Every time I saw another black columnist come out and join the ridicule chorus, as you did . . . it grieved me. The folks your alter ego accurately calls "the unlettered black masses" suffer so much, and take so much undeserved contempt and abuse. It is just not appropriate to add insult to this injury by showering ridicule, contempt, and abuse on the structurally interesting dialect they happen to speak. I was really sorry that virtually every columnist in the USA chose nonetheless to do just that. (Pullum, personal communication, January 1997)

Raspberry never replied. Pullum's explanations and examples were clear and easy to understand. A person capable of thinking rationally about language diversity ought to have accepted them and corrected his erroneous representation of the linguistic abilities of a large segment of the African American population. The problem, however, is that Raspberry, an African American himself, and many other Americans do not think rationally about Ebonics. That is why the statement and restatement of clear, well developed arguments, supported with salient examples and presented by experts, are rejected by so many intelligent people.

Lesson #8—Many people believe that it is acceptable to ridicule and to make jokes about Ebonics and other nonstandard varieties of English.

Courtland Milloy (1996) of the *Washington Post* wrote an enlightened article during the debate entitled, "Nothing's Funny About Ebonics." Given the outpouring of jokes that ridiculed and mocked the dialect and its speakers, Milloy must be one of few people in this country other than language professionals who believes this. The hostile, vicious jokes that were boldly told about Ebonics provided the most powerful evidence that the strategy of disseminating well-researched facts is not working. The facts were drowned out by laughter. Bill Cosby (1997) coined a derisive new name, "Igno-Ebonics." Another well-known African American, Willie Brown, the mayor of San Francisco, incited laughter when he quipped, "I had dinner last night with the mayor of Oakland and had to bring a translator along." (Branson, 1996, p. 2)

Before the debate was over, however, the jokes and mocking assaults, led unfortunately by African Americans, turned painfully cruel for Ebonics speakers. Exploiting the climate of permission to say anything about Ebonics, some jokers shifted the focus from the language to the people. Consider the following event list from the "Ebonic Olympic Games" which appeared on the Internet:

Ebonic Olympic Games Event List

Opening Ceremonies
The Torching of Olympic City
Gang Colors Parade
Track and Field
Rob, Shoot and Run
9MM Pistol Toss
Molotov Cocktail Throw
Barbed Wire Roll
Chain Link Fence Climb
Peoplechase
Monkey Bar Race
100 Yard-Dog Dash (While Being Chased by Police Dogs)
200 Yard Trash Can Hurdles
500 Yard Stolen Car Battery Run
1000 Meter Courtroom Relay (Team of 4 Passing Murder Weapon)
1500 Meter Television Set Relay
1 Mile Memorial Richard Pryor Burning Ether Run
5 Mile High Speed Automobile Chase
Bitch Slapping (Bruises inflicted on wife/girlfriend in three 1 minute
    rounds)
Ebo-Marathon (26 Mile Long Distance Run While Evading Blood
    Hounds)

[http://www.tcnet.net/joe/ebonics.html]

This ruthless parody reeks with undisguised contempt and unbridled racism. The denigration of the people who speak Ebonics is deliberate. The joker's message is clear: Ebonics speakers not only have a bad language, they are bad people—vicious criminals who are comfortable engaging in heinous crimes. It is abundantly clear that presenting research to people like those who created this parody would only squander precious time.

Passionate appeals from distinguished linguistic researchers to end the cruel mockery of the language of Ebonics speakers, many of whom are young children, fell on deaf ears. Walt Wolfram, president of the American Dialect Society and distinguished professor of linguistics at North Carolina State University, who has conducted research on Ebonics for nearly 30 years, appealed to Bill Cosby to end his mockery in a letter to the *Wall Street Journal*. Wolfram (1997) wrote:

> As a dialect expert, Bill Cosby is a great comedian. Unfortunately, the minstrel-like parody of African American Vernacular Speech, or Ebonics, as "Igno-Ebonics" reinforces the most severe racist and classist stereotypes of what linguists know to be a highly intricate, patterned language system. As a public figure, Bill Cosby has a national forum for his opinion. That ought to be taken seriously rather than abused with misinformed, stereotypical caricature which ironically violates the systematic integrity of the dialect he mocks derisively—and the stated goals of the Oakland program . . . I challenge Mr. Cosby to be responsible to his public stature and talk to the language scientists in the linguistics department at his alma mater, the University of Massachusetts, about what he obviously missed in Linguistics 101. I predict that he will follow the lead of Jesse Jackson, who withdrew his sharp criticism of the Oakland resolution after meeting with genuine language scientists. (p. 1)

The *Wall Street Journal* never published Professor Wolfram's letter.

Lesson #9—Many people think that the differences between Ebonics and Standard English are minimal and can be learned without formal instruction.

Many people seem to think that Ebonics speakers can learn Standard English without the benefit of formal instruction. Among them is John McWhorter, a professor of linguistics at the University of California at Berkeley. In the first of *The Black Scholar's* two issues devoted to Ebonics, McWhorter (1997a) claimed: "It is a fact that Black English is not different enough from standard English to pose any significant obstacle to speaking, reading, or writing it" (p. 9). In *The Black Scholar's* second issue on Ebonics, McWhorter restated his position more emphatically: "To suppose that black children cannot negotiate the one-inch gap between their home dialect and standard English . . . insults their intelligence" (1997b, p. 2). The evidence is abundant, however, that thousands of intelligent students do not learn to close that gap. One of them is Michael Lampkins, who was a high school senior and student director on the Oakland School Board at the time of the debate. Commenting on the Oakland resolution in his Senate testimony, he noted:

> When a student doesn't understand the teacher and the teacher does not understand the student, learning does not take place . . . We do have teachers who have went into the classrooms not having the capability to understand those students and have classified those students as special education. (*Ebonics*, 1997, p. 1)

This accomplished and highly regarded student used a nonstandard verb phrase, "have went," that is common among speakers of Ebonics. Formal instruction on the rules that govern the irregular verbs of Standard English would be very useful for him.

Another student who has not learned to close the gap is Maurice White, a sophomore at Oakland Technical High School at the time of the debate. Responding to a fellow student's recommendation to give the Ebonics proposal a chance to be implemented, Mr. White said this:

> Ebonics should not exist . . . Aside from teachers teaching standard English, them just talking about Ebonics means the slang will start coming out the teacher's mouth just 'cause they trying to help kids get it right. (Evans, 1997, p. A17)

Perceiving and learning the differences between the syntactic, semantic, and phonological features that distinguish Ebonics from SE are not easy tasks for some speakers. This is the reason that so many never succeed in learning SE as a second dialect. To minimize and trivialize the many differences between SE and Ebonics, even though both dialects share the same basic vocabulary, is misleading and unfair to Ebonics speakers. This trivialization impedes progress toward recognizing and accepting the fact that many need formal instruction in order to learn SE.

The Afrocentric scholar and founder of Kwanzaa, Dr. Maulana Karenga ("Dr. Karenga speaks," 1997), also commented on the problems that Ebonics speakers face when there is no formal instruction in SE.

> When a child is in a math class you don't interrupt him to tell him, "Say 'are' instead of 'is,' or 'is' instead of 'are.' " Can you imagine interrupting a chemistry class to stop an Asian for saying "valy" instead of "vary" because "l" and "r" are transposed in the language? What is the purpose of that? A linguistic discussion in the midst of chemistry class? They are not doing it to educate us, they are doing it to devalue us . . . they are not only devaluing our speech, they are devaluing our people and our culture.

Karenga highlights the urgent need to provide formal instruction in Standard English for Ebonics speakers.

Lesson #10 —Many people believe that federal and state funds should not be used to pay for Standard English instruction for Ebonics speakers.

Almost everyone believes that all students who speak Ebonics should be required to learn SE. However, an important relevation during the debate was that no one wants to pay for their instruction. A disturbing number of politicians acted swiftly to introduce legislation that would prohibit the use of tax dollars for providing SE classes for Ebonics speakers. Leading the legislative prohibition was North Carolina Senator Lauch Faircloth, who said "Ebonics is absurd" and "Ebonics is just one more foolish plan by educators who should know better. It's political correctness that has gone out of control" ("Senate Mulls," 1997). New York Representative Peter King (R-Seaford), a staunch supporter of making Standard English the federal government's official language, was another politician who introduced legislation that would bar the use of federal funds to help Ebonics speakers learn SE. He revealed his ignorance and contempt for the variety when he claimed that "Ebonics is a verbal stew of inner-city street slang and bad grammar—it is not a language" (Evans, 1997, p. A17). Others who introduced legislation were California Senator Ray Haynes (R-Murieta), Virginia delegate L. Preston Bryant, Jr. (R-Lynchburg), and lawmakers in Georgia and South Carolina.

Although no official request had been made for money, Secretary of Education Richard Riley announced that school districts that recognize Ebonics in their teaching cannot do so with federal funds targeted for bilingual education. This position was maintained even after the Oakland School Board clarified its position and stated that it did not intend to apply for federal money to fund programs that teach SE. Secretary Riley refused to listen to the language professionals who could have helped him make an informed decision about what is required to teach SE to Ebonics speakers. This, unfortunately, provides another example of the failure of spreading accurate information.

Lesson #11—Many people ignore and even ridicule language experts when they present the facts about Ebonics.

Like many other linguistic scholars, I was invited to appear on a number of television and radio shows during the Ebonics debate. Their producers stressed that the purpose was to provide linguistic expertise and clarity for the public. I was stunned by the responses of many talk show hosts and members of the audience to my carefully selected linguistic examples that provided incontrovertible evidence that Ebonics is a systematic and rule-governed language. Most people flatly rejected the evidence. Some, like Bob Novak, one of the hosts on CNN's "Crossfire," which is shown all over the world, rejected my evidence and ridiculed it. After a rather heated discussion on Ebonics with Oakland School Board member Toni Cook and me, Novak said this to his cohost, Bill Press:

> Bill, for the first time that we have been together—agreeing (sic). I'm terribly depressed and I'm depressed to find two well educated women giving this *gobbledygook* [emphasis added] and not saying that they can teach these kids what is proper English so they can get along in this very tough economy and tough environment they're going into . . . And the depressing thing is . . . we have spent money all over the country on this pseudo language, pseudo

dialect when we're so short of money to teach these kids things they really need for survival in a tough society and in a tough economy. (Cable News Network, January 3, 1997)

Bill Press closed the show with these remarks.

And by the way, tell them they're wrong when they're wrong and it's not going to hurt their feelings and if it does, hey, that's part of growing up, Bob. From the left, I be Bill Press. Good night for Crossfire. (Cable News Network, January 3, 1997)

I was dumbfounded! The linguistic ignorance, the power to spread that ignorance, and the arrogance of these two men were breathtaking.

Other people's reactions to the linguistic experts were similarly dismissive. For example, African American sociologist Julia Hare and I appeared as guests on Geraldo Rivera's Ebonics show (March 4, 1997), also watched by millions of people. During the show, I attempted to support my position for the Oakland Board's revised resolution by indicating that the Linguistic Society of America had passed a resolution approving the Board's proposal. Ms. Hare looked at me squarely and said, "Oh, they are nothing but a bunch of linguistic missionaries."

At least one person, Jesse Jackson (he may have been the only one), did listen to the experts and dramatically changed his position about Ebonics and the Oakland Board's resolution. At the beginning of the debate, Reverend Jackson had criticized harshly the resolution by saying, "I understand the attempt to reach out to these children, but this is an unacceptable surrender, borderlining on disgrace . . . It's teaching down to our children" (Lewis, 1996). Jackson's criticism indicates that he, like many people, thought the Board had proposed to *teach* Ebonics. However, after a meeting with Oakland school officials and advisors that clarified the intent of the Board's proposal, Jackson changed his position and endorsed Oakland's plan. He pointed out that "they're not trying to teach black English as a standard language . . . They're looking for tools to teach children standard English so they might be competitive" (Davidson, 1996, p. A6).

It was disturbing that Reverend Jackson was actually criticized for changing his position after meeting with Oakland officials. A number of columnists commented negatively on the leader's reversal. Rob Morse (1997) sneered, "For a few days it was fun listening to Jesse Jackson do 180s on the subject" (p. A3) of Ebonics; and Louis Menand (1997), writing in the *New Yorker*, said Jackson "has a knack for entering as a conciliator in controversies he himself helped stir up" (p. 4). To my knowledge, Jackson received no praise for acknowledging his misinterpretation of the issues and his subsequent decision to change his position after meeting with the experts. My impression is that most people were far more comfortable with Jackson's original position, which denigrated Ebonics, than they were with his later, more enlightened position.

It was disheartening to observe that many people who denigrated Ebonics were granted the status of experts during the debate. This was the case for Armstrong Williams, a conservative, nationally syndicated columnist and television talk show host. Mr. Williams was one of only a dozen people who were invited to testify at the Senate hearings on Ebonics. Here is an excerpt from his testimony.

> The controversy and the tumult surrounding Oakland School Board's proposal to use "Ebonics" as a means of teaching standard English deeply troubles me . . . [b]ut even more troubling to me is what I think is a misguided approach to education in this country. . . . I have with me here my editorial assistant . . . who was born and raised a short distance from here in Southeast Washington—I remember him telling me that when he attended Ketchum Elementary School in Anacostia, his mother constantly corrected his broken English, not allowing him or his brother to make a habit out of speaking his neighborhood slang. (*Ebonics*, 1997)

Armstrong Williams was *invited* to testify, in spite of the fact that he probably has never taken even an elementary course in linguistics. How did he qualify to provide testimony along with distinguished linguistic experts like Dr. Orlando Taylor, Professor and Dean of the Graduate School of Arts and Sciences at Howard University; Dr. William Labov, Professor of Linguistics at the University of Pennsylvania; and Dr. Robert Williams, Professor Emeritus of Psychology at Washington University and the scholar who coined the term *Ebonics*? Clearly someone with the power to select the witnesses liked what Williams had to say about Ebonics, in spite of the fact that his message was uninformed. When I called Senator Specter's office and asked to be a witness, I was told that all of the witnesses had been selected. The distinguished Stanford University linguistic researcher John Rickford was also rejected as a witness; he had to submit his testimony in the form of a support letter. The witness selection process for the Ebonics hearings provides another telling example that we need to do so much more than publicize research findings to surmount the obstacles facing Ebonics speakers.

Lesson #12—The intricate relationships between language and power in the United States are hidden from most people.

The only way that we can explain many of the reactions to Ebonics is to consider the complex relationships between language and power, and the standard language ideology in this country. In his masterful discussion of these relationships, the British linguist Norman Fairclough noted that language is "being increasingly caught up in domination and oppression" (1989, p. 4). For speakers of Ebonics and their ancestors, this was the case right from the beginning. The domination and oppression started during slavery and continues to this very day, although not to the same degree. Slave owners, the dominant group, used language as a calculated tool of oppression when they separated slaves who spoke the same language. The obvious goal of this ruthless act of language planning was to prevent communication among the slaves that might result in a successful insurrection and the end of domination by the slave masters. John Baugh's (1998) analysis is correct: Ebonics is indeed "the linguistic consequence of the slave trade."

Another powerful domination tactic during slavery was the strict prohibition against teaching slaves to read and write. In their comprehensive discussion of slave codes during the colonial period, Franklin and Moss (1994) noted:

> For major offenses . . . slaves were to receive sixty lashes and be placed in the pillory, where their ears were to be cut off. For petty offences, such as insolence and associating with whites and free blacks, they were to be whipped, branded, or maimed . . . Under no conditions were [slaves] to be taught to read and write. (pp. 58, 62)

For slaves and their descendants, the impact of the prohibition against formal instruction in reading and writing, which lasted nearly 200 years in some states, was inestimable. It supported the evolution and development of the linguistic rules that speakers use to generate modern-day Ebonics. There is no evidence of a group of illiterate people anywhere in the world who succeeded in learning a standard language before they had the opportunity to learn to read and write.

As the slave codes indicate, the dominant group exercised power over the slaves and their language through the use of coercion, including physical violence. Today this subordination tactic is prohibited, but the dominant group maintains linguistic power by employing the less transparent tactic of manufacturing consent (Fairclough, 1989). This involves convincing the subordinate group to accept the standard language ideology, which Lippi-Green (1994) defines as "a bias toward an abstracted, idealized, homogeneous spoken language which is imposed from above, and which takes as its model the written language. The most salient feature is the goal of suppression of variation of all kinds" (p. 166).

The standard language ideology is pervasive and deeply entrenched in the United States. The dominant group has succeeded in achieving almost unanimous consent that Ebonics is bad and should be rejected, and that Standard English is good and should be the only acceptable variety. Discussion of the other lessons has indicated that subordination tactics are employed to suppress the use of Ebonics and other nonstandard varieties of English. Chief among these during the debate were mockery, ridicule, and derogatory labeling.

Now we can explain why Bill Cosby, a person who is deeply committed to the empowerment of African Americans, would parody Ebonics. He has accepted the standard language ideology. While Mr. Cosby's support of African American causes and institutions has been unfailing, he, like almost everyone else in this country, is unable to see the extent to which his assumptions about SE and Ebonics have been shaped by relations of power between the dominant group and the subordinate one. Other African Americans—some prominent, like Maya Angelou, Kweisi Mfume, Jesse Jackson, and some not so prominent—could not see these relations either. (It is important to note again that Jesse Jackson changed his position regarding Ebonics.) Perhaps that is why everyone was laughing so uproariously at Ebonics jokes when there is nothing funny about using a group's language as a tool to degrade and deride them, to malign their intelligence and their moral character, and to continue their oppression.

Acceptance of the standard language ideology by well educated African Americans should not be entirely puzzling. Conforming to the standards (for language and many other behaviors) set by the dominant group has been a requirement for survival, literally. Conformity was a requirement during slavery, with its strict, brutal, and coercive codes, and it is a requirement today, although the codes related to language rely more on consent than coercion. Comments during the debate about the need to speak Standard English in order to get a job elucidate this point.

> Black English may suffice on the streets of Oakland and other big cities. But don't expect it to get you into college or land you a well-paying job. For that only standard English will do. ("A Pitiless Hoax," 1996, p. B6)

This position was articulated in a *San Diego Union-Tribune* editorial and was supported by Albert Shanker (1997), president of the 900,000-member American Federation of Teachers, who noted that the Oakland Board members

> recognized that people who want to be successful in American society must be proficient in mainstream English. Many of Oakland's African-American students are not, and they are at a disadvantage when they try to get jobs or further education.

In her article, "Ebonics Is Black-on-Black Crime," Karen Hunter (1997) criticized leaders for not stressing the importance of the relationship between getting a good job and speaking Standard English.

> The Oakland school board, and the handful of New York leaders who jumped on the Ebonics bandwagon . . . claim to be concerned with making poor black children "feel better." . . . But how good will that kid feel when the only job he can hold down is at McDonald's? "Would you like fries with that?" (p. 41)

Finally, Bill Cosby (Groer & Gerhart, 1997) used another parody to express his views on the need to speak Standard English in order to get a job.

> I was at a fund-raiser for Morehouse College. . . . Some speakers called it Mo'house and some said Morehouse. Being the smart aleck that I am, I got up and said I wish someone would explain for me, please, the difference. The school president explained . . . "The difference between Morehouse and Mo'house is that the ones that already have a job say Mo'house." (p. C3)

In spite of the possibility of an empty promise, Ebonics speakers and their descendants have waged a valiant struggle to conform to the standard language patterns. Failure to conform could indeed cost them a job, and if there is no job, there is no food, no shelter, and possibly no life. We should not be surprised then that so many African Americans embrace and cling to the standard language ideology. They are convinced that it is necessary for their survival. The poet June Jordan's warning captures this explicitly.

> The powerful don't play; they mean to keep that power, and those who are the powerless (you and me) better shape up/mimic/ape/ suck-in the very image of the powerful, or the powerful will destroy you—you and our children. (1985, p. 138)

Lesson #13—A relatively small but persistent chorus of voices has resisted the subordination of Ebonics for more than 30 years, and they continued this resistance during the debate.

The coining of the term Ebonics 25 years ago was a bold act of resistance initiated by the Black psychologist Robert Williams (1975) at a conference he convened on cognitive and language development in the Black child. During the conference, attended by both Black and White scholars, Williams met separately with the Black scholars, who were frustrated and angry about the fact that White scholars dominated the research on Black English. It was then that the term *Ebonics* was coined. Williams (1997) reported:

> I coined the term ebonics . . . I had grown sick and tired of White linguists writing about the language of African Americans. Their descriptions of our language were "substandard speech," "restrictive speech," "deviant speech," "deficient speech," "nonstandard English," "Black English," and so on in this negative fashion. . . . My

language is me. It is an extension of my being, my essence. It is a reflection and badge of my culture. Criticism of my language is essentially a direct attack on my self-esteem and cultural identity. (p. 209)

I am not aware of any evidence that shows that White linguists used the terms "deviant" and "deficient" to describe Ebonics, but many nonlinguists certainly did. Williams's anger stemmed from the fact that others had control over describing his language and deciding what to call it. Thus the naming process for the psychologist and his colleagues represented a conscious and determined act of resistance to the dominant group's power to name another group's language. Williams noted:

The African American scholars and I decided that we needed to become self-determined and take over this issue and name our language. We must name and define our reality rather than let others do that for us." (1997, pp. 209-210)

Many people believe that the selection of the new name was a glib act, as evidenced by the jokes about it and by Margo Jefferson's claim that it is pretentious:

Let's call it Black English instead of ebonics. Americans can never resist inventing pretentious names for new schools of thought, new religions or aspiring new disciplines: euthenics, Dianetics, ebonics. (1997, p. C11)

The invention of the name Ebonics was overtly and highly political. It represented a deliberate rejection of all of the names designated by scholars from the dominant group. Apparently Margo Jefferson was totally unaware of the complex race and class issues that provided the motivation for renaming the language variety spoken by many African Americans.

The Oakland Board's resolution, which sparked the debate, represents another act of resistance to the subordination of Ebonics. In spite of the fact that the first version contained language that was confusing and misleading, the Board's proposal to teach African American students Standard English without devaluing Ebonics, the language that many speak at home, is revolutionary. The content of the proposal indicates that the Oakland Board rejected the standard language ideology propagated so successfully in this country; the Board members refused to consent to the notion that Ebonics is bad and thus has no place in the classroom.

Other examples of resistance include the tireless efforts of language professionals, specifically the many linguists and speech-language pathologists who have been disseminating the facts about Ebonics through publications, conference presentations, and workshops for more than three decades. At the height of the debate. the 6,000-member Linguistic Society of America (LSA) issued a resolution that supported the Oakland School Board's proposal. Drafters of the resolution articulated in clear and convincing language a restatement of facts about Ebonics.

> The variety known as "Ebonics," "African American Vernacular English" (AAVE), and "Vernacular Black English" and by other names is systematic and rule-governed like all natural speech varieties. In fact, all human linguistic systems—spoken, signed, and written—are fundamentally regular. The systematic and expressive nature of the grammar and pronunciation patterns of the African American vernacular has been established by numerous scientific studies over the past thirty years. Characterizations of Ebonics as "slang," "mutant," "lazy," "defective," "ungrammatical," or "broken English" are incorrect and demeaning. (Linguistic Society of America, 1997)

The LSA's resolution was followed by another resolution disseminated by the 90,000-member American Speech–Language–Hearing Association (ASHA):

> The current debate over whether Black English is a dialect or a second language is not new to . . . ASHA . . . which addressed the controversy 13 years ago and formally recognized Black English, or "Ebonics," as a separate social dialect with systematic and highly regular linguistic features. . . . ASHA . . . recognizes Ebonics as one of many linguistic varieties including standard English, Appalachian English, southern English, New York dialect, and Spanish influenced English. ASHA . . . also contends that no dialectal variety of English is a disorder or a pathological form of speech or language and that

each variety serves a communication function as well as a social solidarity function.

Finally, one scholar in the African American intellectual community, linguist Geneva Smitherman, has engaged in an extraordinary effort to resist the subordination of Ebonics. Dr. Smitherman uses Ebonics to write portions of her books and articles for academic journals. In a recent article entitled "Black Language and the Education of Black Children: One Mo Once," Smitherman (1997) wrote:

> When the Oakland School Board tapped into the Ebonics framework, they were seeking an alternative pedagogical paradigm to redress the non-education of black youth in their school district. We should applaud their refusal to continue doing more of the same that has not worked in the past. *Speaking of which, how come ain none of dese black so-call "leaders" raise no sand bout the lack of literacy among black youth? Seem to me dat's where they ought to be puttin they energy instead of doggin those Oakland school folk!* [emphasis added] (p. 29)

The last two sentences are replete with phonological and syntactic features characteristic of Ebonics: the use of the double negative "ain none"; the use of "bout" that exhibits the absence of the unstressed initial syllable *a*; the use of "dese" and "dat's," which exhibits the *d* sound instead of the *th* sound; the use of *in* instead of *ing* in *puttin* and *doggin*, and the use of the regularized form of the possessive pronoun *they* instead of *their*.

In many publications, including her first book on Ebonics, *Talkin and Testifyin: The Language of Black America*, Smitherman (19771986) writes in both SE and Ebonics, boldly rejecting all of the appropriacy arguments (Fairclough, 1992; Lippi-Green, 1997) put forth by proponents of the standard language ideology. Dr. Smitherman has the courage to practice what she preaches: Ebonics is just as good as SE, and it can be used for the same purposes as SE. Smitherman is in a class by herself; I know of no other linguist or SLP who has this kind of professional courage. Many of us have accepted the appropriacy arguments; thus we would not be comfortable writing academic documents in Ebonics, and most important, we are too afraid that our work might not get published if we wrote in that dialect. As Lippi-Green noted, the threats are real.

The Need for a New Strategy

The lessons learned from the Ebonics debate—and there are many—have revealed with disturbing consistency the colossal failure of the research dissemination strategy. Repeating, for more than three decades, the well-researched facts about Ebonics in distinguished, scholarly, impassioned, and energetic voices has not changed the American people's assessment of the dialect. The lessons learned provide overwhelming evidence that the majority of the people in the United States still believe that Ebonics is a pseudo-language, street language, slang, junk, gibberish, verbal stew, broken English, a joke, or just plain old bad English that needs to be corrected. It is futile to continue repeating the facts about Ebonics. We are already hoarse from continually screaming a linguistic message that almost no one wants to hear, let alone accept. Michele Foster (1997) pointed out

> that most pundits had already decided what they believed; they were saying, "Don't confuse me with the facts, I've already made up my mind." And they wouldn't change their minds even if they were presented with the linguistic facts, because the controversy over Ebonics is about more than language; it is about politics. (p. 7)

Another strategy is urgently needed to help Ebonics speakers overcome the longstanding and crippling educational, social, and economic problems caused by the public's erroneous and contemptuous assessment of their language. We, the language professionals—linguists and speech-language pathologists in particular—have a responsibility to develop and implement a new, successful strategy. We owe this to Ebonics speakers. These speakers have given us so much; we have used their language to build our professional careers. The time is ripe for us to give something back—something substantial, as Rickford (1997) articulated so persuasively in his splendid but guilt-provoking article, "Unequal Partnership: Sociolinguistics and the African American Speech Community."

The task of developing and implementing a viable new strategy has been made less daunting for everyone because John Baugh has already completed some of the groundwork. Baugh presents a compelling argument for a bold new strategy that would involve classifying Ebonics speakers as language minority speakers. This would make them eligible for federal funds that could be used to pay for formal instruction in Standard English. Baugh (1998) argued:

> The term "language minority" is too narrowly defined under current regulations, and . . . a revised definition is needed in support of reforms that seek to provide high academic standards for all students; indeed, this need has been accentuated by the Ebonics controversy. . . . We need language policies that will ensure that students who are *not native speakers of standard English* [emphasis added] will not fail due to linguistic neglect. The status quo is one that favors students who arrive at school speaking standard American English. . . . Unless systemic reforms take adequate account of the dynamics of linguistic diversity among students we are unlikely to meet our desired goal to combine high academic standards with greater educational equity for all.

Baugh also argued that classifying Ebonics speakers, who are nonnative speakers of Standard English, as language minority students is justified because of their unique linguistic history:

> Slave descendants have a unique linguistic history . . . when compared to every other group that has migrated to the U.S. As forced immigrants . . . slaves did not have the linguistic luxury of a gradual transition to English. Whereas the typical European immigrant came to the U.S. with fellow speakers of their native language, slaves were linguistically isolated upon capture; that is, whenever possible. Whereas the typical European immigrant was able to maintain a family, slaves had no such right; as chattel they were subject to immediate sale; a practice that destroyed many black families. Whereas the typical European immigrant was able to attend public schools, slaves were denied education by law, and after emancipation, were subject to inferior education under strict policies of educational apartheid.

No one likes to talk about slavery; it was such a brutal, painful, dehumanizing, and sad chapter in our history. But Baugh is correct; it is essential that we take this history into full consideration, especially the language and education part of it, when searching for strategies to surmount the linguistic barriers that Ebonics speakers face. The time is long overdue for this country to acknowledge that it created the circumstances that gave rise to and sustained Ebonics. The United States has a responsibility to help Ebonics speakers add Standard English to their repertoires. This country owes these speakers formal instruction in Standard English, and yes, federal funds should be used to pay for it, contrary to the opinion of racist legislators. Americans cannot feign innocence and pretend that Ebonics speakers talk the way they do because they are "too lazy" to speak "correctly." This may be an expedient excuse to further suppress Ebonics speakers, but it is another blatant falsehood. Baugh has already proposed a new, well-motivated classification system that is based on the necessary and sufficient evidence for categorizing Ebonics speakers as a language minority group. His reformed categorization scheme highlights and justifies the need for federal funds. In Orlando Taylor's testimony during the Senate hearings on Ebonics, he also stressed the need for federal support for Ebonics speakers. He told Senator Specter that the federal government should

> provide funds and incentives for local school boards to upgrade the skills of the current teacher force to teach standard English to culturally and linguistically diverse learners [and] [p]rovide funds to support research and dissemination on "best practices" to teach standard English to African American and other children that do not speak standard English as their primary language system. (*Ebonics*, 1997)

If Americans are serious about the linguistic empowerment of Ebonics speakers, they will have to pay for them to learn Standard English. It is imperative that the people in this country recognize this essential fact. Language professionals have a key role to play, for we must provide the leadership required to change the educational policies so that they reflect an expanded definition of language minority students. Baugh has argued convincingly that the new definition should include all nonnative speakers of Standard English. The enormous task of changing the relevant educational policies will not be easy or accomplished quickly. However, if we do not commit ourselves to completing this task and solving the oppressive language-related problems that Ebonics speakers have endured for so long, we will have no defense, as language professionals, when we are placed in the shameful category of imprudent, short-sighted Americans described by Randall Robinson (1998):

> American decision makers, who walk the power corridors of media, government, industry, and academia, are characterized by a blissful and self-serving forgetfulness. When the great global and domestic problems that beset our society are divorced form their derivation or history, public policymakers do not feel constrained to attend to such problems before or beyond the predictable intermittent flare-up. Like impressive dreams that cannot be recalled moments after waking, Americans quickly forget about the crises whose evolution they never studied to begin with. The [Ebonics controversies], the Somalias, the South Central L.A.'s, the Three Mile Islands—with the loss of media interest these dissolve quickly from all pubic memory. Policymakers then without solving much of anything, move on to the next lighted stage. (p. 125)

The Ebonics controversy was, indeed, a lighted stage, but some of us will not move on. We are committed to solving the problems that were illuminated, once again, by the debate. The lessons learned offer critical insights that can be utilized to help solve the longstanding problem of providing appropriate language assessments for Ebonics speakers.

References

Abu-Jamal, M. (1997). The mother tongue: Black English revisited. *Black Scholar, 27*(1), 26-27.

Baugh, J. (1998). Linguistics, education and the law: Educational reform for African American language minority students. In S. Mufwene, J. Rickford, G. Bailey, & J. Baugh (Eds.), *African American English* (pp. 282-301). London: Routledge.

Bowman, R. (1997, January 13). Ebonics earns a failing grade. *Washington Times*, p. C5.

Boyd, H. 1997. Been dere, done dat! *Black Scholar, 27*(1), 15-17.

Branson, A. (1996, December 26). Beltway crowd weighs in on Oakland School Board's talk of Black English. *Legis-Slate News Service*. (Available: www.legislate.com)

Cable News Network. (1997, January 3). *Crossfire—Ebonics debate.*

Charen, M. (1997, January 2). Is street slang a distinct language? *Detroit News*, p. A7.

Cleaver, E. (1997, February 4). Ebonics belongs in the streets. *Newsday*, p. A36.

Cosby, B. (1997, January 10). Elements of Igno-Ebonics style. *Wall Street Journal.*

Datcher, M. (1997, January 13). Black English: An issue of pain and pride. *The Athens News.*

Davidson, R. (1996, December 31). Jackson shifts stance on Black English effort. *Washington Post*, p. A6.

DeWitt, K. (1996, December 29). Ebonics, language of Richard Nixon. *New York Times*, sec. 4, p. 3.

Dr. Karenga speaks on Ebonics debate. (1997, March 3). *Long Beach Union*, pp. 2-3.

Ebonics: Hearing before the Subcommittee on Labor, Health and Human Services, and Education, of the Senate Committee on Appropriations, 105th Cong., 1st Sess. 54 (1997) (testimony of Michael Lampkins).

Ebonics: Hearing before the Subcommittee on Labor, Health and Human Services, and Education, of the Senate Committee on Appropriations, 105th Cong., 1st Sess. 68 (1997) (testimony of Orlando Taylor).

Ebonics: Hearing before the Subcommittee on Labor, Health and Human Services, and Education, of the Senate Committee on Appropriations, 105th Cong., 1st Sess. (1997) (testimony of Armstrong Williams).

Evans, M. (1997, January 13). Locally, few favor movement. *Newsday*, p. A17.

Fairclough, N. (1989). *Language and power*. London and New York: Longman.

Foster, M. (1997). Ebonics and all that jazz: Cutting through the politics of linguistics, education, and race. *The Quarterly, 19*(1), 7-12.

Franklin, J., & Moss, A., Jr. (1994). *From slavery to freedom: A history of African Americans.* New York: McGraw-Hill.

Groer, A., & Gerhart, A. (1997, January 8). Bill Cosby, standing up for the caucus. *The Washington Post*, p. C3.

Harris, J. (1996, December 25). U.S. bilingual education funds ruled out for Ebonics speakers. *Washington Post*, p. A2.

Hunter, K. (1997, January 17). Ebonics is Black-on-Black crime. *New York Daily News*, p. 41.

Jefferson, M. (1997, January 7). The two faces of Ebonics: Disguise and giveaway. *New York Times*, p. C11.

Jordan, J. (1985). Nobody mean more to me than you and the future life of Willie Jordan. *On call: Political essays* (pp. 123-139). Boston: South End.

Labov, W. (1972). Academic ignorance and Black intelligence. *The Atlantic Monthly, 229,* 59-67.

Lewis, N. A. (1996, December 23). Black English isn't a second language, Jackson says. *New York Times,* p. B9.

Linguistic confusion. (1996, December 24). *New York Times,* p. A10.

Linguistic Society of America. (1997, January). *LSA resolution on the Oakland "Ebonics" issue.* (Available: www.lsadc.org/web2/ebonicsfr.htm)

Lippi-Green, R. (1994). Accent, standard language ideology, and discriminatory pretext in the courts. *Language and Society, 23*(2), 163-198.

Lippi-Green, R. (1997). *English with an accent: Language, ideology, and discrimination in the United States.* London and New York: Routledge.

McGrory, M. (1996, December 29). The GOP's Newt-bonics. *Washington Post,* p. C1.

McWhorter, J. (1997a). Wasting energy on an illusion. *The Black Scholar, 27*(1), 9-14.

McWhorter, J. (1997b). Wasting energy on an illusion: Six months later. *The Black Scholar, 27*(2), 2-5.

Menand, L. (1997, January 13). Johnny be good: Ebonics and the language of cultural separatism. *The New Yorker,* pp. 4-5.

Milloy, C. (1996, December 29). Nothing's funny about Ebonics. *Washington Post,* p. B1.

Morse, R. (1997, January 3). 1996: E coli, Odwalla, ebola, ebonics. *San Francisco Examiner,* p. A3.

Pitiless hoax: Ebonics hinders learning standard English. (1996, December 23). *San Diego Union-Tribune,* p. B6.

Raspberry, W. (1996, December 26). To throw in a lot of "bes," or not? *Washington Post,* p. A27.

Rich, F. (1997, January 8). The Ebonic plague. *Wall Street Journal.*

Rickford, J. (1997). Unequal partnership: Sociolinguistics and the African American speech community. *Language in Society, 26,* 161-1997.

Robinson, R. (1998). *Defending the spirit: A Black life in America,* New York: Dutton.

Rowan, C. (1996, December 25). "Ebonics" a false promise of self-esteem. *Chicago Sun-Times.*

Senate mulls Black English as teaching aid. (1997, January 23). *Yahoo News Reuters Limited.*

Shanker, A. (1997, January 5). Where we stand: Ebonics. [American Federation of Teachers advertisement]. *New York Times.*

Smitherman, G. (1986). *Talkin and testifyin: The language of Black America.* Detroit: Wayne State University. (Original work published 1977)

Smitherman, G. (Ed.). (1981). *Black English and the education of Black children and youth.* Detroit: Wayne State University Center for Black Studies.

Smitherman, G. (1997/1986). Black language and the education of Black children: One mo once. *Black Scholar, 27*(1), 28-35.

Sneider, D. (1996, December 23). Black English in Oakland Schools: Slang or language. *Christian Science Monitor,* United States, p. 1.

Weiss, R. (1997, January 6). Among linguists, Black English gets respect. *Washington Post,* p. A10.

Will, G. (1997, January 2). An example of problem solving. *The San Diego Union-Tribune,* p. B12.

Williams, P. (1996, December 29). The hidden meaning of Black English. *New York Times,* sect. 4, p. 9.

Williams, R. (1975). *Ebonics: The language of Black folk.* St. Louis: Center for Black Studies.

Williams, R. (1997). The Ebonics controversy. *Journal of Black Psychology, 23,* 208-214.

Wolfram, W. (1997, January 11). [Challenge to Bill Cosby]. Unpublished letter to the *Wall Street Journal.*

Young, Billie J. (1991). Fannie Lou Hamer: This little light of mine . . . . In D. Abbott (Ed.), *Mississippi writers: Reflections of childhood and youth: Vol. IV. Drama* (pp. 516-530). Jackson: University of Mississippi Press.

Testimony of Orlando L. Taylor on the Subject of "Ebonics"

United States Senate Committee on Appropriations
Subcommittee on Labor, Health and Human Services
and Education
The Honorable Arlen Specter, Chairman
Thursday, January 23, 1997

Mr. Chairman and Distinguished Members of the Subcommittee:

Let me begin by thanking you for having the foresight to schedule a special hearing on language issues and academic underachievement of many of our nation's African American children. I am honored to have been invited to present testimony on this very important subject. To my knowledge, this hearing is the first that the Congress of the United States has ever called specifically to address this issue.

This special hearing comes in the wake of several weeks of controversy and debate in the nation's news media on the subject of Ebonics, a learned, social dialect that is at variance with standard American English and one that is spoken by many—but certainly by no means all—African Americans. This sometimes emotionally laden controversy has been, in my view, divisive and frequently characterized by misinformation and misconceptions.

While the controversy has raged, one central fact remains and that is that far too many African American children have not acquired sufficient proficiency in standard English to facilitate academic success and career mobility. Many of these children speak as their primary language system a rule governed, social dialect of English referred to variously as Ebonics, African American English, Black English, Black English vernacular, African American Language Systems, etc. This variety of English, as other nonstandard English dialects, has often been stigmatized by the mainstream society. Yet it often has currency among peers, family, and community as an acceptable means of communication, especially in informal situations.

Moreover, Ebonics, as well as elements of African American urban slang (a different aspect of African American communication), have been popularized—indeed glamorized—in the nation's popular culture through film, television, and recorded music. It is indeed somewhat paradoxical that Ebonics and other aspects of African American communication are devalued in some aspects of American life, but used as a legitimate vehicle for generating millions of dollars in other aspects. On the other hand, this phenomenon reinforces perhaps the commonly held sociolinguistic principle that there is a time and place for all language.

In any event, I believe that our challenge as a nation is to devise positive, sensitive, and effective ways to teach African American and other children standard English—the language of education and career mobility. In my opinion, such instruction should be delivered in an environment that (1) does not denigrate the student, (2) recognizes that all groups have a human right to retain culturally based language systems to communicate with family, peers, and friends, and (3) utilizes the language systems that children bring to school as a vehicle for teaching them the school's language. After all, "taking students where they are to where they need to go" is an educational principle that is as American as apple pie.

The current Ebonics debate, while fueled by a resolution passed by the Oakland Unified School District, revolves around several long standing issues. However, the Oakland proposal to use students' language as a vehicle to teach standard English is neither new, nor limited to Oakland. Similar programs have been in existence, and often funded by local, state, or Federal (Title I) funds, for more than two decades. In California alone, similar programs are currently in operation in 17 school districts (see appended list). One in Los Angeles reportedly enrolls approximately 20,000 of the district's 93,000 African American children. Similar programs have been initiated in such diverse locations as Atlanta, Georgia; Dallas, Texas; Miami, Florida; and Seattle, Washington.

Many academic topics have been—and will continue to be—examined and debated by sociolinguistic scholars. These topics include such issues as the nature of language systems spoken in the African American community, their origins, what to call them, and whether to classify them as languages or as dialects. These healthy academic discussions should be encouraged and funded by the Federal government through its various research programs designed to understand the nature and history of the American people.

However, these academic pursuits should not—indeed must not—cause us to blur our sights on the larger goal of how to teach standard English to all of our nation's children and yet celebrate their diversity and their ability to communicate effectively in a variety of settings.

As our schools seek to achieve this goal, we must be ever mindful of certain generally accepted facts about the way English is spoken in the United States. Some of these facts are appended to this testimony. I would like, however, to highlight just five of the most salient of these facts:

1. Many African American children come to school communicating in a language system that diverges from standard English. This language system has been well described as a rule governed system that is deeply rooted in a variety of complex social, political, economic, historical, and educational factors. This language system may be spoken by children as well as adults and should not be confused with African American slang, although many users of these language systems may also speak African American slang.

2. African American children are not the only children that may come to school speaking a nonstandard regional or social dialect. Thus, the current Ebonics issue is not solely an African American issue, but rather one that probably typifies the language situation for many other groups of American children. It is reasonable to expect that these children are also at risk for low academic achievement.

3. There is a difference between slang and dialect. While many media reports and public commentaries on the Oakland School Board's proposals have focused on contemporary African American slang, the Oakland program focuses upon the finite set of pronunciation and grammatical dialect rules that govern the speech of many— again not all—working class African Americans. Slang is rapidly changing vocabulary and idioms used by certain "in-groups" within a culture.

4. Using the language that children bring to the classroom as a bridge to teaching new language systems is a widely used technique in second language instruction.

5. Competence in more than one language or dialect makes one more effective in communicating with a variety of groups.

Mr. Chairman and distinguished subcommittee members, the current Ebonics controversy has brought us face to face with a quintessential American issue. That is, how can we as a nation accommodate, indeed celebrate, linguistic diversity, while at the same time teach children to speak, write, read and comprehend standard English—the language system that will facilitate cohesion among our nation's diverse groups and facilitate access to achievement and careers for all students.

I wish to respectfully suggest that this national question needs Federal direction and support. Specifically, I believe that the Federal government should:

• Provide incentives and support to the nation's colleges and universities to produce the next generation of teachers with a better knowledge of cultural and linguistic diversity, and the skills required to effectively teach standard English to increasingly diverse student bodies. Such instruction should be delivered in a positive environment that celebrates diversity and encourages communication that fits the audience and situation. In many ways, this may be one of the greatest imperatives for the United States. As our nation's population becomes increasingly diverse (already upwards of 1/3 of the population are members of racial and cultural minorities), it is absolutely essential for our schools to teach all students the language skills that are needed for access to further learning in mathematics, engineering, the humanities, and the physical, biological, and social sciences. Indeed, I believe that our nation will have a difficult time retaining its status as a world power if it does not accomplish this goal.

• Provide funds and incentives for local school boards to upgrade the skills of the current teacher force to teach standard English to culturally and linguistically diverse learners.

• Provide funds to support research and dissemination on "best practices" to teach standard English to African American and other children that do not speak standard English as their primary language system. Many individuals have doggedly insisted upon using traditional methods for teaching standard English to African American children that devalue the language systems that many of them bring to school. Yet, the facts show that these approaches have simply failed in far too many instances. If they had been more successful, we would have no need for this current hearing.

Many individuals, including myself, have argued for an approach to teaching standard English that utilizes the language brought to school by children as a bridge—a base if you will—to teach standard English. This approach is based upon the assumptions that there is a time and place for all language, that the role of schools is to extend, enhance, and deepen language skills and that versatility in language usage is an asset.

Federal support is needed to assess and document the effectiveness of this and other alternative strategies to teach standard English. I am confident that African American children are fully capable of acquiring competence in standard English. However, they must be motivated to do so, believe (along with their teachers) that they can do so, and taught it in a positive environment free of ridicule and denigration.

• Provide support for our nation's colleges and universities to produce more research on the diverse language and communication systems used by African Americans and other culturally diverse groups across the spectra of gender, age, education, region, and socioeconomic status. To date, most of the research on African American communication has focused on the working classes, and the results of that research have been overgeneralized to the entire African American community.

It has often been said that progress often evolves out of debate and controversy. I believe that the current Ebonics controversy has given our nation an opportunity to engage in thoughtful discourse, leading to the institution of new policies and practices to address one of our most challenging national issues. As I have said, it is clearly in the nation's best interest to produce children who can speak, read, write and comprehend standard English in order to be competitive in the information age, and yet at the same time preserve the rich cultural heritages of our people. I believe that we can, and indeed that we must, do both.

Finally, we must do a better job in educating the public on language issues. The current Ebonics flap has been fueled by considerable misinformation. Too many stereotypes continue to exist about the language and communication of African Americans and other culturally diverse groups of Americans. We need to inform our citizens about the true nature—and value—of linguistic diversity among our citizens, and that this diversity means in no way that we must lower our standards in teaching standard English. Indeed, through this recognition of diversity, we may come closer to achieving our goal of successfully teaching standard English to all of our children, and in so doing, provide them with the tools for greater academic achievement. Clearly our nation will win in such a situation. And, our children—all of them—will most certainly win as well.

Some Generally Accepted Sociolinguistic Facts

1. Variations within English—or any language—are normal, learned phenomena that exist as regional and social dialects. These variations result from a complex mix of social, political, historical, and economical factors. These dialects have been described by a number of distinguished scholars and such august professional societies as the Linguistic Society of America and the American Speech-Language-Hearing Association. The linguistic system referred to by some linguists as Ebonics is a vernacular English variety. It may be spoken in a number of social situations by some African Americans, but especially among the underclass, the undereducated, and the socially isolated.

2. Vernacular language systems are often devalued within societies, e.g., the Cockney of England, the English of the Appalachian mountains, Brooklynese in New York City—and Ebonics!

3. All language systems are learned, not biologically based.

4. It is absurd for schools to teach Ebonics or any other vernacular language system. It is highly unlikely that any school system in the United States has ever made teaching Ebonics or any other vernacular dialect as a goal. Using the vernacular language system brought to school by children as a bridge to teaching the school's language cannot be equated with teaching the vernacular language.

5. Teachers don't have to speak Ebonics or any other vernacular language in order to teach standard English. However, it is desirable for them to understand the rules of these systems if they are to use them as bridges to teach standard English.

California School Districts With Standard English Proficiency Programs That Address the Language Learning Needs of African American Children

Center Unified School District
Compton Unified School District
Del Paso Heights Unified School District
Duarte Unified School District
Grant Unified School District
Los Angeles Unified School District
Lynwood Unified School District
Oakland Unified School District
Pomona Unified School District
Ravenswood Unified School District
Richmond Unified School District
Sacramento Unified School District
San Bernardino Unified School District
San Francisco Unified School District
Stockton Unified School District
Vallejo City Unified School District
West Fresno Unified School District

Some Suggested Readings

Baugh, J. (1983). *Black street speech: Its history, structure and survival.* Austin: University of Texas Press.

Dillard, J. L. (1972). *Black English: Its history and usage in the United States.* New York: Random House.

Fasold, R. (1984). *The sociolinguistics of society.* London: Basil Blackwell.

Rickford, J. R. (1987). *Dimensions of a creole continuum.* Stanford, CA: Stanford University Press.

Saville-Troike M. (1982). *The ethnography of communication.* Baltimore: University Park Press.

Taylor, O. L. (1986) Teaching standard English as a second dialect. In O. Taylor (Ed.), *Treatment of communication disorders in culturally and linguistically diverse populations.* Austin, Texas: Pro-Ed.

About the Editors

Carolyn Temple Adger is a program associate at the Center for Applied Linguistics (CAL) in Washington, DC, where she conducts research on teaching and learning in linguistically diverse schools. With Walt Wolfram, she led a project that developed equitable speech/language assessment procedures for speakers of African American Vernacular English in a large city school system. Her classroom research includes a study of how instructional activity influences students' dialect choices, reported in *Kids Talk: Strategic Language Use in Later Childhood* (Hoyle & Adger, 1998). She also co-authored *Dialects in Schools and Communities* (1999).

Donna Christian is president of the Center for Applied Linguistics (CAL), where her research focuses on the role of language in education, including issues of second language education and dialect diversity. Among her research projects are studies (with Walt Wolfram) of Appalachian English, Ozark English, American Indian English, and Vietnamese English. She has co-authored *Appalachian Speech* (1976); *Variation and Change in Geographically Isolated Speech Communities: Appalachian and Ozark English* (1988); *Dialects and Education* (1989); and *Dialects in Schools and Communities* (1999).

Orlando Taylor is dean of the Howard University Graduate School of Arts and Sciences and graduate professor in the School of Communications. He is president of the National Communication Association. He has written books, articles, and monographs in the fields of communication disorders, sociolinguistics, educational linguistics, and intercultural communication. These include *Treatment of Communication Disorders in Culturally and Linguistically Diverse Populations* (1986); and (with Patricia A. Cole) "Performance of Working Class African-American Children on Three Tests of Articulation" in the July 1990 issue of *Language, Speech, and Hearing Services in Schools*.

About the Authors

John Baugh is professor of education and linguistics at Stanford University. His research and teaching focus is on the educational and policy implications of linguistic science. He is currently engaged in collaborative research with the Oakland Unified School District regarding programs for adult educational advocates of elementary school students. He has published extensively on matters pertaining to language usage among African Americans, culminating with the publication of *Out of the Mouths of Slaves: African American Language and Educational Malpractice* (University of Texas Press, Austin, 1999).

Courtney Cazden is the Charles William Eliot Professor of Education Emerita at Harvard University. Her writings related to this book include *Subcultural Differences in Child Language: An Interdisciplinary Review* (1966); *Making It and Going Home: The Attitudes of Black People Toward Language Education* co-authored with B. H. Bryant and M. A. Tillman (1970); and *Functions of Language in the Classroom,* co-edited with V. J. Steiner and D. Hymes (1972), which was a response to the dialect research of the 1960s. She is now writing a second edition of her book, *Classroom Discourse* (1988).

Kelli Harris-Wright is coordinator for Title I federal programs in the DeKalb School System, Decatur, Georgia, where she supports and supervises classroom teachers, designs curriculum, and teaches professional development classes. She holds a B.S. in speech language pathology and audiology from Tennessee State University and an M.A. in speech language pathology and audiology from Kent State University. She was the 1988 recipient of the Louis M. DiCarlo Award from the American Speech-Language-Hearing Association for the state of Georgia for developing the Bidialectal Communication Instructional Model.

Dr. Asa G. Hilliard III is the Fuller E. Callaway Professor of Urban Education at Georgia State University, with joint appointments in the Department of Educational Policy Studies and the Department of Educational Psychology and Special Education. He has published extensively on testing, Ancient African history, African culture, and child development. His most recent books are *The Maroon Within Us: Selected Essays on African American Community Socialization* and *SBA: The Reawakening of the African Mind.*

Terry Meier is associate professor of education at the Wheelock College Graduate School in Boston. She has written numerous articles on teaching literacy to Ebonics-speaking students, including "Never So Truly Free: Reading and Writing About Malcolm in the Community College," in *Teaching Malcolm X* (Perry, 1996); and "Kitchen Poets and Classroom Books: Literacy From Children's

Roots" and "Teaching Teachers About Black Communications," both in *The Real Ebonics Debate* (Perry & Delpit, 1998).

John R. Rickford is the Martin Luther King Centennial Professor of Linguistics and African and Afro-American Studies at Stanford University. He is also director of the Program in African and Afro American Studies and president of the International Society for Pidgin and Creole Linguistics. His numerous scholarly articles include "Suite for Ebony and Phonics" in *Discover* magazine (December 1997). His published books include *Analyzing Variation in Language* (co-editor, 1987) and *African American English* (co-editor, 1998). He is currently authoring a book of essays on African American Vernacular English, co-authoring (with Russell J. Rickford) *Spoken Soul: The System, Source and Significance of the African American Vernacular*, and co-authoring (with Lisa A. Green) a textbook, *African American Vernacular English and Its Contexts*.

Geneva Smitherman holds the title of University Distinguished Professor of English at Michigan State University, where she also directs "My Brother's Keeper," a middle school mentoring program. She is author of over 100 articles on language, culture, and education, and author or editor of eight books, including *Talkin & Testifyin: The Language of Black America* (1977/1986) and *Black Talk: Words and Phrases From the Hood to the Amen Corner* (1994).

Anna F. Vaughn-Cooke is dean of the School of Graduate Studies and Research at Florida A & M University. She holds a master's degree in speech–language pathology from the University of Maryland and master's and doctoral degrees in linguistics from Georgetown University. She has conducted studies on language change in African American Vernacular English, and her article on the Divergence Hypothesis is considered a critical contribution to the sociolinguistics literature. During the Ebonics controversy in 1997, she provided expert linguistic commentary for more than 20 television and radio shows, including CNN's "Crossfire," "The Geraldo Rivera Show," and Bev Smith's show on Black Entertainment Television (BET).

Walt Wolfram is the William C. Friday Distinguished Professor at North Carolina State University, where he directs the North Carolina Language and Life Project. In addition to his research program on the dialects of North Carolina, he is actively engaged in teaching middle school students about their community dialects. Each year, he spends two weeks teaching eighth graders in North Carolina about their dialect heritage. His published books include *American English: Dialects and Variation* (1998).

Language in Education: Theory and Practice

Language in Education: Theory and Practice is the monograph series of the ERIC Clearinghouse on Languages and Linguistics. The *LIE* series covers topics in foreign language education, English as a second language, bilingual education, language variation, adult ESL literacy, refugee and immigrant education, and child language acquisition. The following *LIE* titles are available from Delta Systems Co., Inc.

- *Adult Biliteracy in the United States*
- *The American Bilingual Tradition*
- *Approaches to Adult ESL Literacy Instruction*
- *Assessing Success in Family Literacy Projects*
- *Cooperative Learning: A Response to Linguistic and Cultural Diversity*
- *ESL Through Content-Area Instruction: Mathematics, Science, Social Studies*
- *Foreign Language Assessment in Grades K-8: An Annotated Bibliography of Assessment Instruments*
- *From the Classroom to the Community: A Fifteen-Year Experiment in Refugee Education*
- *Immigrant Learners and Their Families: Literacy to Connect the Generations*
- *Literacy and Language Diversity in the United States*
- *Making Meaning, Making Change: Participatory Curriculum Development for Adult ESL Literacy*
- *Profiles in Two-Way Immersion Education*
- *Talking Shop: A Curriculum Sourcebook for Participatory Adult ESL*
- *Through the Golden Door: Educational Approaches for Immigrant Adolescents with Limited Schooling*
- *Writing Our Lives: Reflections on Dialogue Journal Writing with Adults Learning English*

Order from

Delta Systems Co., Inc.
1400 Miller Parkway
McHenry, IL 60050
1-800-323-8270 (in Illinois call 1-815-363-3582)
http://www.delta-systems.com

Out-of-print titles in the series have been archived in the ERIC database of educational materials and can be ordered on microfiche or in hard copy from EDRS. For a complete list of titles, contact ERIC/CLL (see page 180).

ERIC Document Reproduction Service (EDRS)
7420 Fullerton Road, Suite 110
Springfield, VA 22153-2852
1-800-443-3742
http://edrs.com

ERIC: Educational Resources Information Center

The Educational Resources Information Center (ERIC) is a nationwide information network that aims to improve educational practice by providing ready access to current, high-quality education literature. ERIC maintains the world's largest database of education-related materials. The ERIC database is available worldwide via the Internet, CD-ROM, and monthly printed indexes.

ERIC also provides direct assistance to those seeking information on education through its network of subject-specific clearinghouses, each of which offers a question-answering service and provides a wide range of free and low-cost publications on current topics in education.

The ERIC Clearinghouse on Languages and Linguistics (ERIC/CLL) collects and disseminates information related to foreign language education, the teaching and learning of English as a second language, bilingual education, and all aspects of linguistics. In addition to the *Language in Education series*, ERIC/CLL publishes a semiannual newsletter, the *ERIC/CLL News Bulletin*; a quarterly electronic newsletter, *Language Links*; a series of 1500-word information digests on current topics in language education; one-sheet minibibliographies; and online resource guides.

ERIC/CLL is operated by the Center for Applied Linguistics, a private non-profit organization, with funding from the National Library of Education of the U. S. Department of Education's Office of Educational Research and Improvement.

Further information on the publications, services, and other activities of ERIC/CLL can be obtained via mail, telephone, e-mail, or our Web site.

ERIC Clearinghouse on Languages and Linguistics
4646 40th Street NW
Washington, DC 20016-1859
800-276-9834
202-362-0700, ext. 204
eric@cal.org
http://www.cal.org/ericcll